2ND EDITION

QUALITIES OF
effective
teachers

JAMES H. STRONGE

**Association for Supervision and
Curriculum Development**

Alexandria, Virginia USA

Association for Supervision and Curriculum Development
1703 N. Beauregard St. • Alexandria, VA 22311-1714 USA
Phone: 800-933-2723 or 703-578-9600 • Fax: 703-575-5400
Web site: www.ascd.org • E-mail: member@ascd.org
Author guidelines: www.ascd.org/write

Gene R. Carter, *Executive Director;* Nancy Modrak, *Director of Publishing;* Julie Houtz, *Director of Book Editing & Production;* Leah Lakins, *Project Manager;* Reece Quiñones, *Senior Graphic Designer;* Circle Graphics, *Typesetter;* Sarah Plumb, *Production Specialist*

All Web links in this book are correct as of the publication date below but may have become inactive or otherwise modified since that time. If you notice a deactivated or changed link, please e-mail books@ascd.org with the words "Link Update" in the subject line. In your message, please specify the Web link, the book title, and the page number on which the link appears.

Paperback ISBN: 978-1-4166-0461-7 • ASCD product: 105156 s01/07
Also available as an e-book through ebrary, netlibrary, and many online booksellers.
(see Books in Print for ISBNs)

Quantity discounts for this book: 10–49 copies, 10%; 50+ copies, 15%; for 500 or more copies, call 800-933-2723, ext. 5634, or 703-575-5634.

Library of Congress Cataloging-in-Publication Data

Stronge, James H.
   Qualities of effective teachers / James H. Stronge. — 2nd ed.
      p. cm.
   Includes bibliographical references and index.
   ISBN-13: 978-1-4166-0461-7 (pbk. : alk. paper)
   ISBN-10: 1-4166-0461-8 (pbk. : alk. paper)   1. Effective teaching.   2. Teacher effectiveness.
I. Title.

LB1025.3.S789 2007
371.102—dc22

   2006028422

12 11 10 09 08 07   12 11 10 9 8 7 6 5 4 3 2 1

To my wife, Terri, a gifted teacher of young children,

and

to devoted teachers everywhere

QUALITIES OF
effective
teachers

2ND EDITION

Acknowledgments

The creation of a project is never an isolated endeavor. This was certainly true in the development of this book. To move from imagination to culmination required the encouragement, support, and assistance of many individuals. I take this opportunity to acknowledge the contributions of many friends, generous colleagues, and capable students.

Colleagues from the College of William and Mary continued to offer invaluable support as the second edition of the book and related projects unfolded. In particular, Patricia Popp, Thomas Ward, and Virginia McLaughlin offered technical support and encouragement for this research. I am indebted to those who assisted on the first edition upon whose work the foundation for the second edition was built. Many of my graduate students contributed significantly to the first edition. Christine Hill, Jeanne Struck, and Kimberly Chandler assisted with a review and synthesis of extant research related to effective teaching. Catherine Little helped refine the conceptual framework and develop an early draft for the manuscript. William Brown, Jennifer Hindman, and Linda Hutchinson worked extensively on the annotated bibliography included in the book. And Lisa Vernon and Jennifer Hindman, again, provided invaluable assistance in refining and editing a final version of the manuscript.

Several of my current and former doctoral students are due enormous credit for their background research, careful editing, and updating of the second edition of *Qualities of Effective Teachers*. In particular, Sheila Ashley, Matthew Edinger, Tamra Freeman, and Trina Spencer, all doctoral students in the School of Education at the College of William and Mary, reviewed research and literature with regard to the qualities of effective teachers, both in general education and with at-risk students. Catherine Little (University of Connecticut), Christine Hill (Newport News Public Schools, Newport News, VA), and Kimberly Chandler (Center for Gifted Education, College of William and Mary) assisted in reviewing and refining the sections on teachers of gifted students. Jennifer Hindman (Teacher Quality Resources, LLC) provided a careful and thoughtful final review of the entire manuscript. I wish to acknowledge the invaluable contributions made by Leslie Grant (Teacher Quality Resources, LLC) to this second edition. She is the contributing author for the new sections in chapters 1 through 6 related to teachers of at-risk students and teachers of high-ability students. Leslie worked tirelessly identifying and synthesizing research to be added to the book, and then editing and refining the final manuscript for publication. I am, indeed, privileged to work with such outstanding current and former doctoral students.

Colleagues from Taylors Elementary School in the Greenville County Public Schools, South Carolina, generously contributed their time and expertise to reviewing and enhancing the teacher responsibilities and teacher behaviors section of the book. In particular, I wish to thank Principal Vaughan Overman, instructional coaches Jean Dickson and Melodie White, and teachers Lois Maxwell Childs and Vicki Sloop for their careful review and enhancements.

To everyone who contributed, I wish to express my admiration for your dedicated work as educators and my appreciation for helping to make this project a reality. And, finally, I wish to acknowledge you, the readers, who embraced the original edition of *Qualities of Effective Teachers,* and thus made this updated version worth the effort. Thank you.

Introduction

The focus of this book is the teacher. The content is presented within the context of a person—the teacher—as opposed to viewing teaching skills as isolated processes. The book is research-based, and the style and format are designed to be user-friendly, providing easy-to-use summaries and tools for teacher effectiveness. In building on the framework provided in the first edition, this new edition provides an update on research related to effective teaching. Added features in the second edition include a focus in each chapter on the qualities to emphasize when working with both at-risk and high-ability students.

If finding or becoming an effective teacher were simple, this book would not be needed. If a single method for developing an effective teacher existed, such a teacher would be in every classroom. Nonetheless, there are common attributes that characterize effective teachers.

Teachers have a powerful, long-lasting influence on their students. They directly affect how students learn, what they learn, how much they learn, and the ways they interact with one another and the world around them. Considering the degree of the teacher's influence, we must understand what teachers should do to promote positive results in the lives of students with regard to school achievement, positive attitudes toward school, interest in learning, and other desirable outcomes. This understanding should be based both on what experts and stakeholders think teachers should do and on what education research has shown to be significant in the preparation and practice of effective teachers.

The second edition of *Qualities of Effective Teachers* chronicles the common background and identifies the common behaviors that characterize effectiveness in the classroom. Although most of what we know about effective teachers in general applies to teachers of at-risk children and children who are identified as gifted in some way, additional teacher qualities, dispositions, and behaviors emerged in a careful review of the extant literature. Based on a comprehensive review and synthesis of research related to effective teaching, this book serves as a resource for teachers, administrators, and others interested in improving the quality of teaching and learning in our schools.

Defining an Effective Teacher

When we consider the complex task of teaching, *effectiveness* is an elusive concept. Some researchers define teacher effectiveness in terms of student achievement. Others focus on high performance ratings from supervisors. Still others rely on comments from students, administrators, and other interested stakeholders. In fact, in addition to *effective,* we vacillate on just how to refer to successful teachers. Cruickshank and Haefele (2001) noted that good teachers, at various times, have been called *ideal, analytical, dutiful, competent, expert, reflective, satisfying, diversity-responsive,* and *respected.*

A teacher's influence is far reaching, so it is challenging to define what outcomes might show effectiveness and how those outcomes should be measured. In addition, many variables outside the teacher's control also affect each of the potential measures of effectiveness.

Despite these complexities, and regardless of what we call them, we can agree that effective teachers do have an extraordinary and lasting impact on the lives of students. In recent years, as the field of education has moved toward a stronger focus on accountability and on careful analysis of variables that affect educational outcomes, the teacher has proven time and again to be the most influential school-related force in student achievement. Consequently, to develop an understanding of what teachers do to cause significant student learning, researchers have begun to focus on the specific characteristics and processes used by the most effective teachers.

The growing body of research on teacher effectiveness has reinforced the notion that characteristics and behaviors matter in teaching, in terms of student achievement as well as other desirable outcomes. Although looking across studies yields some inconsistencies in defining elements of effectiveness, careful exploration of the research, nevertheless, helps confirm which practices are most important and which require further investigation. Commonalities highlighted in the second edition of *Qualities of Effective Teachers* include characteristics of the teacher as an individual; teacher preparation; classroom management; and the way a teacher plans, teaches, and monitors student progress. Put these jigsaw pieces together, and a portrait of an effective teacher takes shape.

New Feature

An addition to the second edition of *Qualities of Effective Teachers* is the focus on teachers of at-risk and high-ability students. Although discussed separately, many students may fall into both categories (Cline & Schwartz, 1999; Manning & Baruth, 1995). Students with high abilities can also be at risk of school failure. Likewise, students at risk of school failure can possess exceptional abilities. Teachers of both high-ability students and at-risk students, like teachers of all students, must take into account the unique needs and characteristics of their students (Struck & Little, 2003). The next two sections discuss some of the variables that place children at risk or describe children with exceptional abilities.

Focusing on At-Risk Students

The term "at risk" has been used in education circles for many decades, but it first entered the public arena in 1983 as a result of the report titled *A Nation at Risk* (National Commission on Excellence in Education, 1983). In general, we think of students as being at risk when they require remediation, are more likely to be retained, are at higher risk of dropping out of school, and have substandard basic skills (Slavin, Karweit, & Madden, 1989).

A study of the graduation rate in California serves as an example. During the 2002–03 school year, students who were deemed "high performing" graduated at a much higher rate than students labeled "low performing." In fact, 30 percent more high-performing students graduated than did low-performing students. Thirty-nine percent of Latinos, 47 percent of African Americans, 67 percent of whites and 77 percent of Asian Americans graduated in 2002. The report stated, "California's failure to graduate so many of its students is a tragic story of wasted human potential and tremendous economic loss" (Civil Rights Project, 2005, p. 6).

Many factors lead to a student's being labeled at risk, including personal, familial, societal, and in-school factors. Societal and familial factors include poverty, discrimination, parenting education, student mobility, television watching, amount of reading in the home, and a host of others (Barton, 2003; Kober, 2001; Manning & Baruth, 1995).

Students from low socioeconomic backgrounds enter school less ready to learn than students from the highest socioeconomic backgrounds. For example, only 39 percent of students living in poverty recognize the letters of the alphabet as compared to 85 percent of students from the highest socioeconomic level (Neuman, 2003). These students face challenges before they enter school.

We know that select school characteristics also can affect a child's education and the risk of a student dropping out of school, repeating a grade, or needing some type of remediation. These school-related factors include the following:

• A less rigorous curriculum in which instruction is watered down and access to more rigorous curriculum is limited.

• A school climate in which students feel that teachers and staff do not expect them to succeed or a climate in which students do not feel safe.

• A segregation of students in which high concentrations of minority and poor students go to school in buildings in disrepair (Kozol, 2005).

Perhaps most germane to the discussion in this book, a key at-risk factor is a teacher who is less experienced, less prepared, and less qualified to teach. In fact, "A salient characteristic of at-risk schools is that they generally have relatively few well-qualified teachers" (National Partnership for Teaching in At-Risk Schools, 2005, p. 6).

Although the picture drawn here is bleak, by no means is it suggested that effective, dedicated, and well-qualified teachers do not exist for at-risk students. In many schools facing a variety of the societal and school characteristics described above, there are teachers shining as beacons who help students achieve academically and who tap into a child's curiosity and motivation to learn. These beacons persist under difficult circumstances, providing stability for students for whom school may be the most stable part of their lives.

Given the importance of addressing the learning needs of at-risk students, a section in each chapter focuses on the teacher of students who, through societal or school factors, are placed at risk for school failure. Although the majority of the literature regarding effective teaching in general applies to teachers of at-risk students, some aspects warrant further discussion and exploration. In fact, current research studies reveal that there are various characteristics of effective teachers of at-risk students that distinguish them from ineffective teachers.

Focusing on High-Ability Students

Simply defining a high-ability learner is a challenge, as well as a matter on which there is not full agreement in the field of education. High-ability learners are referred to as gifted, talented, creative, independent thinkers, complex thinkers, leaders, emotionally intense, and curious. This list is certainly not exhaustive but demonstrates that one definition of "giftedness" upon which most educators, researchers, parents, and students can agree may not exist (Baska, 1989; Reis & Small, 2001; Vaughn, Bos, & Schumm, 2000). Hence, we use the term "high ability" to connote both identified gifted students and those high-achieving students who have not been formally identified as gifted. High-ability learners generally have been characterized as having—and exhibiting—a high degree of one or more of the following qualities:

- General intellectual ability
- Specific academic aptitude
- Creative or productive thinking
- Leadership ability
- Visual or performing arts ability
- Psychomotor ability (VanTassel-Baska & Little, 2003)

In addition to the list above, other types of giftedness or intelligence have been explored, including Howard Gardner's Theory of Multiple Intelligences, which is built upon the premise that students may be not just mathematically or verbally talented but also talented athletically, musically, and interpersonally, to name a few (Gardner, 1983). Regardless, students with high ability in some area need access to a teacher who recognizes their unique abilities and works with these students to enhance their talents in a multitude of ways. Nearly 40 years ago, Joseph Renzulli, a leader in the field of gifted education, stated that the teacher is the most important element in the success of programs for gifted students (Renzulli, 1968).

Unfortunately, access to highly effective teachers in programs that serve high-ability students is inconsistent at best. A study of 100 eminent persons revealed that these individuals *could not* identify a teacher who influenced them or who, they perceived, played a role in their educational development. Secondary school, in particular, brought negative memories (Csikszentmihalyi, Rathunde, & Whalen, 1993). A study of women who dropped out of mathematics or engineering programs at the college level revealed that the majority did so because of poor teachers (Brainard & Carlin, 2001). Conversely, a study of 125 talented people revealed that teachers did play a role in their development (Bloom, 1985). This inconsistency leads to some students excelling and reaching their potential while some drop out of school or fail to pursue the development of their talents.

The role of the teacher of gifted or high-ability students is a critical one. Research regarding what works and what doesn't with the general student population does not address some of the important elements of effective teaching in the gifted classroom or in the mixed-ability classroom where differentiation of instruction is used to meet the range of needs. As with teachers of at-risk students, we devote a new section in each chapter to defining qualities of effective teachers of high-ability learners.

Overview

The second edition of *Qualities of Effective Teachers* sheds light on the elusive concept of teacher effectiveness by summarizing research results accumulated across several decades to define specific teacher behaviors that contribute to student achievement and other measures of effectiveness. The book was developed by focusing specifically on the *teacher* and his or her preparation, personality, and practice, rather than on other influences such as student demographics, school and district administration, or organizational decision making outside the teacher's control. The sources considered in creating this synthesis of teacher background and behaviors include broad-based studies of teacher practice as linked to student achievement, case studies of teachers identified as effective within specific contexts, surveys and interviews among stakeholders, meta-analyses of teacher effectiveness studies, and other reviews of research.

The research findings and recommended practices identified in this book should seem like old friends to many teachers. For these effective teachers, the book is a review that serves as a reminder for continued improvement. For others, the same findings serve to build awareness as they take steps to enhance their effectiveness. By focusing on teacher effectiveness, our ultimate goal is to improve the educational experiences and achievement of the students we serve in our schools.

Organization of the Book

The second edition of *Qualities of Effective Teachers* is designed to serve as a resource and reference tool for educators. It identifies elements of effective teaching within broad categories and points readers interested in further exploration to the research studies and reviews used in the preparation of the text. The book is divided into two parts. Part 1 focuses on the research useful in developing a profile of what an effective teacher is, and Part 2 contains myriad resources

The first two chapters explore the teacher as an individual and as a professional. Chapter 1 investigates prerequisites of effective teaching, focusing on the influence of a teacher's background and professional preparation. The implications of verbal ability, content knowledge, educational coursework, and teacher certification are explored. Chapter 2 examines what the effective teacher is like as a person, focusing on a teacher's nonacademic interactions with students and on the aspects of a teacher's behavior that make him or her loved, respected, and remembered by students as personally effective. This chapter also explores the significance of the teacher's professional attitude. This discussion emphasizes dedicated and reflective practice among effective teachers.

Chapters 3 through 6 focus more specifically on aspects of a teacher's job responsibilities and practices. Chapter 3 considers the management and organizational skills that an effective teacher displays, with emphasis on establishing an effective learning environment in which routines and discipline are established and maintained to serve as a backdrop for instruction and student engagement. Chapter 4 investigates organization for instruction with a focus on maximizing the amount of time allocated for instruction, communicating expectations for student achievement, and planning for instructional purposes. Chapter 5 focuses on implementing instruction with an emphasis on communication and complexity of instructional content by using appropriate questioning techniques and supporting active learning. Chapter 6 examines monitoring student progress and potential through discussing the importance of homework and applying findings of student learning outcomes, as well as responding to and meeting the individual needs of special populations within the classroom.

Within each chapter, information is organized into categories of characteristics or behaviors that are supported by the existing research as important aspects of teacher effectiveness. Summaries of research are provided in a straightforward manner in each chapter, with a list of key references to guide the interested reader to further information on the topics. Chapter 7 contains a brief conclusion on what an effective teacher is and how teacher effectiveness can be improved, with additional thoughts regarding teachers of at-risk students and teachers of high-ability learners.

Part 2, the final section of the text, includes teacher skills assessment checklists, behaviors to look for in effective teacher performance, an annotated bibliography of selected sources, and a complete reference list. This portion of the book focuses on helping teachers improve, whether the need for improvement is self-diagnosed or the result of supervisor assistance. In particular, the checklists and qualities should be helpful in converting research findings into more effective practice. The checklists have been updated to include selected salient qualities of teachers of at-risk and high-ability learners. These qualities are an addendum to the already existing qualities for teachers in general.

Uses for the Book

By closely aligning the attributes of high-quality teaching with curricula and assessments, we can be better equipped to identify links between classroom processes and desirable student outcomes. Thus, the second edition of *Qualities of Effective Teachers* is aimed at improving the quality of teacher performance and learning opportunities for students. In this effort, the book can be a valuable resource for the following audiences:

• Teachers who desire to improve their own performance through analysis and reflective practice.

• Teacher leaders who are engaged in mentoring, peer coaching, and collaborative schoolwide improvement.

• School administrators and department heads who supervise and evaluate teachers.

• Staff development specialists who plan and deliver training focused on improving instruction for the range of abilities that exist in classrooms.

• Human resource specialists who are responsible for recruiting and selecting high-quality teacher applicants.

• Teacher and administrator educators who can use the book's research syntheses in their teacher training and instructional leadership programs.

• Policymakers and their staffs who are responsible for developing tools and strategies for state or district teacher development and evaluation processes.

Each group contributes to the education of students and has a vested interest in their success.

Related Resources: Archer, 1998; Barton, 2003; Baska, 1989; Bloom, 1985; Brainard & Carlin, 2001; Cawelti, 2004; The Civil Rights Project, 2005; Cline & Schwartz, 1999; Cotton, 1999, 2000; Cruickshank & Haefele, 2001; Csikszentmihalyi et al., 1993; Darling-Hammond, 2000; Gardner, 1983; Kober, 2001; Kozol, 2005; Manning & Baruth, 1995; National Board for Professional Teaching Standards, n.d.; National Commission on Excellence in Education, 1983; National Partnership for Teaching in At-Risk Schools, 2005; Olson, 1997; Reis & Small, 2001; Renzulli, 1968; Slavin et al., 1989; Struck & Little, 2003; Tucker & Stronge, 2005; Vaughn et al., 2000; Wright, Horn, & Sanders, 1997.

Part 1

What It Means to Be an Effective Teacher

Part 1 of *Qualities of Effective Teachers, 2nd Edition* focuses on the research useful in developing a profile of an effective teacher. Following the introduction, the first six chapters of the book address major categories of teacher effectiveness. Chapters 1 and 2 explore the teacher as an individual and as a professional. Chapters 3 through 6 focus on aspects of a teacher's job responsibilities and practices. Finally, Chapter 7 discusses what an effective teacher is and how teacher effectiveness can be improved.

1

Prerequisites for Effective Teaching

For several years, Miriam worked as a paraeducator in a self-contained special education classroom. Everyone who encountered her knew she was an asset to the school, based on the way she worked with students and the professionalism she demonstrated every day in the school. She dressed for the role of teacher, offered thoughtful and informed comments about students, and took an active interest in the school. She was encouraged to complete coursework to earn her special education endorsement. When she did complete her degree a few years later, her principal offered her a teaching contract for the next school year. Miriam is well respected for her knowledge of students with special needs and of how to make appropriate accommodations for them. Most important, she uses her knowledge and expertise daily to benefit the students with whom she works and serves as a resource to the school's administration on issues related to special education.

There is a major educational debate today about how to recruit and prepare teachers. Many educators, policymakers, and taxpayers question whether traditional preservice programs prepare teachers who can maintain excellent instructional programs that increase student achievement. Alternative programs for recruiting and preparing teachers have been devised, giving rise to research comparing the effectiveness of teachers from different types of preparation backgrounds. Beyond the issue of pedagogical preparation, the question of content knowledge and its relevance to effective teaching remains a legitimate concern.

This chapter explores the research on teacher preparation and reviews what has been learned through extensive studies and research regarding the background of effective teachers. Each section of the chapter summarizes research findings related to a specific aspect of a teacher's background.

Figure 1.1, located at the end of the chapter, summarizes the relationships among each of the background aspects described in the chapter and provides the related references.

Verbal Ability and Effective Teaching

Does a teacher's intellectual ability or aptitude translate into improved effectiveness in the classroom? Over several decades, researchers have investigated relationships between teacher ability, as demonstrated through teachers' scores on aptitude tests such as the SAT (Scholastic Assessment Tests) or GRE (Graduate Record Exam), and the achievement of students. The results of such studies have been mixed. Some show no relationship beyond the level of basic skills knowledge; however, other studies have shown connections, particularly in linking teachers' verbal ability with their students' performance.

While research generally has not supported a connection between the teacher's intellectual aptitude and student success, one key finding has emerged: students taught by teachers with greater verbal ability learn more than those taught by teachers with lower verbal ability (see, for example, Rowan, Chiang, & Miller, 1997; Strauss & Sawyer, 1986). Thus, a discernible link exists between effective teachers' vocabulary and verbal skills and student academic success, as well as teacher performance. Because communication skills are a part of verbal ability, teachers with better verbal abilities can more effectively convey ideas to students and communicate with them in a clear and compelling manner.

The following conclusions can be drawn from the research:

• Teachers' scores on tests of verbal ability were the only input found to have a direct positive relationship on student achievement (Coleman et al, 1966).

• Students taught by teachers with high verbal skills perform better on standardized tests than do students taught by teachers with lower verbal ability (Strauss & Sawyer, 1986).

• A positive relationship exists between student achievement and teachers with high verbal ability (Thomas B. Fordham Foundation, 1999; Rowan et al., 1997; Wenglinsky, 2000).

• General intellectual aptitude typically has not been linked to higher student achievement; however, when teachers perform well on basic skills tests, their students also tend to do better on academic measures (Hanushek, 1971).

Related Resources: Andrew, Cobb, & Giampietro, 2005; Darling-Hammond, 2000; Darling-Hammond, 2001; Hanushek, 1971; Haycock, 2000, 2003; Murnane, 1985; National Center for Education Statistics, 1992; Rowan et al., 1997; Thomas B. Fordham Foundation, 1999; Wenglinsky, 2000.

Educational Coursework and Effective Teaching

Teacher preparation has traditionally included a series of courses focusing on child development, instructional and assessment techniques, and methods and materials related to specific content areas; however, in recent years, teacher preparation programs and their usefulness to the teaching field have received considerable scrutiny. Some recommendations and programs for teacher certification have curbed traditional teacher training in favor of brief, more practical and focused preparation of individuals with subject-area degrees and varying backgrounds, including those with military and business training.

Partly in response to these programs, several studies have focused on teacher effectiveness related to the amount and type of educational coursework in a teacher's preparation program. Studies support the finding that fully prepared teachers understand how students learn and what and how they need to be taught. In addition, their background knowledge of pedagogy makes them better able to recognize individual student needs and customize instruction to increase overall student achievement. To illustrate this key point, one study indicated that teachers who completed a five-year teacher preparation program intended to remain in education more often than those who completed a four-year program (Darling-Hammond & Sykes, 2003). Teachers with better professional preparation are also able to provide students with more diverse opportunities to learn.

There is little research regarding the long-term effects of alternatively prepared teachers, but studies indicate that they may have more initial difficulty in the classroom than traditionally prepared teachers (see, for example, Miller, McKenna, & McKenna, 1998). Alternative teacher preparation programs are characterized as condensed versions of traditional preparation routes. A review of fast-track alternative programs found that preservice teachers had less coursework and less time in the field both observing and student teaching (Johnson, Birkeland, & Peske, 2005).

A key factor in the effectiveness of alternatively prepared teachers is the type of experiences within the preparation program. Teachers from alternative preparation programs that provided mentors, clinical teaching experiences, and preparation in pedagogy stated that they felt confident in their teaching abilities and intended to continue teaching (Darling-Hammond & Sykes, 2003). Teachers from fast-track programs wanted more preparation in teaching within their content areas, and they wanted better field experiences (Johnson et al., 2005). Without these components, preservice teachers are ill-prepared to enter the teaching profession. A study of the effectiveness of teachers trained through Teach for America—a program involving five weeks of intense training—revealed that students taught by certified teachers consistently outperformed students taught by Teach for America teachers (Darling-Hammond, Holtzman, Gatlin, & Heilig, 2005). Teachers who are not formally prepared to teach know little about how children grow, learn, and develop, or about how to support learning differences. Teachers with little or no coursework in education consistently have difficulties in the areas of classroom management, curriculum development, student motivation, and specific teaching strategies. They are less able to anticipate student knowledge and potential difficulties, or to plan and redirect the lesson to meet the individual needs of the students.

On the other hand, one strong predictor of teaching performance is the amount of coursework in education. Studies have consistently found positive effects of teachers' formal education training on supervisory ratings and student learning. In addition to educational coursework, content knowledge is important. For example, one study indicated that students' science achievement positively related to teachers' course-taking background in both education and science (Wenglinsky, 2000). A study in mathematics resulted in similar findings (Hill, Rowan, & Ball, 2005). Thus, we can have confidence that both content knowledge and pedagogical skills are vital aspects of teacher effectiveness.

The following points summarize important outcomes related to educational coursework in teacher preparation:

• A teacher's formal pedagogical preparation has been shown to have a positive effect on student achievement, especially in the areas of mathematics, science, and reading (Monk, 1994).

- The teachers who completed programs of study in education consistently perform better on state licensing exams than do teachers who did not attend a program of study in education (Gitomer, Latham, & Ziomek, 1999; Wise, 2000).

- A teacher's subject-matter expertise supports student learning up to a point, but educational coursework appears to have a substantive value-added influence on student achievement (Monk, 1994).

- A positive relationship exists between student achievement and how recently an experienced teacher took part in a professional development opportunity such as a conference, workshop, or graduate class (Hanushek, 1971).

- Teachers prepared in schools of education demonstrate stronger classroom management skills and can better relate content to the needs and interests of students (Ferguson & Womack, 1993).

- The ability to apply and integrate knowledge or skills to a particular population in a specific setting is the key characteristic of an effective teacher (Demmon-Berger, 1986; Mitchell, 1998; Porter & Brophy, 1988).

- Eighth grade students have higher achievement when they have teachers with the following three characteristics: they engage in hands-on learning emphasizing higher-order thinking; they majored or minored in the subject that they teach; and they have training in how to develop higher-order thinking skills (Wenglinsky, 2002).

Related Resources: Ashton & Crocker, 1987; Blair, 2000; Darling-Hammond, 2000, 2001; Darling-Hammond & Sykes, 2003; Druva & Anderson, 1983; Ferguson & Womack, 1993; Fetler, 1999; Hanushek, 1971; Hill et al., 2005; Holt-Reynolds, 1999; Johnson et al., 2005; Mason, Schroeter, Combs, & Washington, 1992; Mathews, 1999; Miller et al., 1998; Monk, 1994; Monk & King, 1994; Schalock, Schalock, & Myton, 1998; Scherer, 2001; Shellard & Protheroe, 2000; Southern Regional Education Board, 1999; Thomas B. Fordham Foundation, 1999; Wenglinsky, 2000, 2002; Wilson, Floden, & Ferrini-Mundy, 2001; Wise, 2000.

Teacher Certification and Effective Teaching

Another important and controversial issue related to the educational preparation of teachers is licensure and certification. In most states, teacher certification status is related to educational background, scores on tests of pedagogical or content knowledge, or both. The No Child Left Behind Act

(2002) defines a "highly qualified teacher" as one who possesses full state certification; however, alternative certification routes are becoming more common, along with alternative recruitment and preparation programs. As with other elements of teacher background, the research findings on licensure and certification related to student achievement are mixed. In fact, one study found that effectiveness among teachers with the same certification status varied more greatly than teachers with varying certifications (Kane, Rockoff, & Staiger, 2006). This suggests that individual teacher quality may be more important than certification type.

Extant research indicates that the number of well-qualified, certified teachers within a state is a consistent and significant predictor of that state's student achievement in math and reading on standardized tests. Some studies concluded that uncertified teachers and out-of-field teachers (i.e., teachers who teach a subject for which they were not prepared) achieve far less with students than do teachers with proper, in-field certification (see, for example, Darling-Hammond et al., 2005; Fidler, 2002). Furthermore, one of the best predictors of low student performance in individual schools is the number of uncertified teachers in the building. Each year, between 10 and 30 percent of new public school teachers begin teaching without full certification. In addition, more than half of the schools in the United States have certified teachers who are teaching in content areas in which they are not certified. One study indicated that this practice of out-of-field teaching actually harms the teacher as well as the students (Ingersoll, 2001). Teachers who are well-qualified in their own fields become ineffective in teaching a subject for which they were not prepared. In fact, teaching a grade level or subject for which a teacher is not certified or has little training may convert a highly qualified and capable teacher into an ineffective one.

In recent years, the National Board for Professional Teaching Standards (NBPTS) has offered a national certification process based on teachers' knowledge of content and pedagogy, the quality of their instructional and assessment practices, and their participation in professional development opportunities. If teachers can demonstrate exceptional abilities in each of these areas through a rigorous portfolio and reflection-based process, they may obtain National Board certification.

To date, research regarding the effectiveness of National Board certified teachers (NBCTs) is mixed, with some studies concluding that students in classrooms led by NBCTs perform better than their peers, and other studies finding limited or no student achievement effects. The authors of selected studies concluded that there is evidence from their studies that National Board certification is related to higher student achievement (Cavalluzzo, 2004; Goldhaber & Anthony, 2004; Vandevoort, Amrein-Beardsley, & Berliner, 2004). For example, in a study of NBCTs and student gains in high school mathematics, Cavalluzzo (2004) concluded, "NBC proved to be an effective signal of teacher quality" (p. 3). Other studies, specifically those conducted by Stone (2002), Stephens (2003), and Stronge and colleagues (2005) have found more mixed results or less conclusive evidence regarding a positive relationship between National Board certification and student achievement.

Some important findings from research related to the overall issue of teacher certification standards and teacher effectiveness include the following:

• Fully prepared and certified teachers have a greater impact on gains in student learning than do uncertified or provisionally certified teachers, especially with minority populations and in urban and rural settings (Darling-Hammond, Berry, & Thoreson, 2001; Goe, 2002; Laczko-Kerr & Berliner, 2002; Qu & Becker, 2003).

• Teacher certification status and teaching within one's field are positively related to student outcomes (Hawk, Coble, & Swanson, 1985).

• Teachers with certification of some kind (standard, alternative, or provisional) tend to have higher-achieving students than do teachers working without certification (Goldhaber & Brewer, 2000).

• Students of teachers who hold standard certification in their subjects score 7 to 10 points higher on 12th grade math tests than do students of teachers with probationary, emergency, or no certification (Goldhaber & Brewer, 2000).

• Some studies have demonstrated relationships between standard certification and teacher practices (e.g., hands-on learning, connections to student experiences) (Darling-Hammond, 2000). These teacher practices have been found to be effective in supporting student achievement, thus illustrating a possible indirect relationship between traditional certification and student achievement.

Related Resources: Cavalluzzo, 2004; Darling-Hammond, 1996, 2000, 2001; Darling-Hammond et al., 2001; Darling-Hammond et al., 2005; Darling-Hammond & Sykes, 2003; Dozier & Bertotti, 2000; Ferguson & Womack, 1993; Fetler, 1999; Fidler, 2002; Goe, 2002;

Goldhaber & Anthony, 2004; Goldhaber & Brewer, 2000; Hawk et al., 1985; Ingersoll, 2001; Laczko-Kerr & Berliner, 2002; Lilly, 1992; Mathews, 1999; Miller et al., 1998; Qu & Becker, 2003; Scherer, 2001; Stronge et al., 2005; Vandevoort et al., 2004; Wise, 2000.

Content Knowledge and Effective Teaching

The role of a teacher's content knowledge has been extensively investigated in the research on teacher effectiveness. Strong content knowledge has consistently been identified as an essential element by those who study effective teaching. Clearly, subject-matter knowledge positively affects teaching performance; however, it is not sufficient in and of itself. Teacher training programs that emphasize content-knowledge acquisition and neglect pedagogical coursework are less effective in preparing prospective teachers than programs that offer both content and pedagogical knowledge.

Studies surveying educational stakeholders about teacher effectiveness place high priority on competence in content knowledge (see, for example, Johnson, 1997). Teachers with subject-matter knowledge are better able to go beyond textbook content and involve students in meaningful discussions and student-directed activities. Some researchers argue that the definition of subject-matter expertise must include the ability to convey and teach content to others, as well as a deep understanding of the concepts and ideas being taught. Additionally, a strong background in content and subject matter assists teachers in planning and organizing lessons that are sequential and interactive.

Investigations of the importance of teacher content knowledge have yielded the following findings:

• Teachers with a major or minor in their content area are associated with higher student achievement, especially in the areas of secondary science and mathematics (Wenglinsky, 2000).

• Students, teachers, principals, and school board members have all emphasized the importance of subject-matter knowledge in describing effective teaching (Covino & Iwanicki, 1996; Johnson, 1997; National Association of Secondary School Principals [NASSP], 1997; Peart & Campbell, 1999).

• The ability to convey content to students in a way that they can grasp, use, and remember is important, but it is not necessarily related to additional teacher knowledge or coursework in the content area (Begle, 1979; Monk, 1994; Monk & King, 1994).

• Content-area preparation is positively related to student achievement within specific subjects, especially in mathematics (Hawk et al., 1985; Wenglinsky, 2002) and science (Druva & Anderson, 1983).

• Several studies have illustrated that teachers with greater subject-matter knowledge tend to ask higher-level questions, involve students in the lessons, and allow more student-directed activities (Wenglinsky, 2000, 2002).

Related Resources: Berliner, 1986; Blair, 2000; Brookhart & Loadman, 1992; Carlsen, 1987; Carlsen & Wilson, 1988; Covino & Iwanicki, 1996; Darling-Hammond, 1996, 2000; Darling-Hammond et al., 2001; Druva & Anderson, 1983; Ferguson & Womack, 1993; Goldhaber & Brewer, 2000; Hill et al., 2005; Holt-Reynolds, 1999; Johnson, 1997; Mitchell, 1998; Monk & King, 1994; NASSP, 1997; National Board for Professional Teaching Standards, n.d.; Peart & Campbell, 1999; Rowan et al., 1997; Shellard & Protheroe, 2000; Shulman, 1987; Traina, 1999; Wenglinsky, 2000, 2002.

Teaching Experience and Teacher Effectiveness

Teaching experience matters in teacher effectiveness and student achievement, at least to a certain point. Experienced teachers differ from rookie teachers in that they have attained expertise through real-life experiences, classroom practice, and time. These teachers typically have a greater repertoire of ways to monitor students and create flowing, meaningful lessons. Teachers who are both experienced and effective are experts who know the content and the students they teach, use efficient planning strategies, practice interactive decision making, and embody effective classroom management skills. These experienced and effective teachers are efficient—they can do more in less time than novice educators can.

Researchers indicate that teachers develop from novices to masters at different rates, taking from five to eight years to master the art, science, and craft of teaching (Darling-Hammond, 2000; Education Review Office, 1998). Therefore, the number of years in front of a classroom may not necessarily indicate whether a teacher is expert. One study suggests that for a teacher to be considered experienced, the ability to apply the "book knowledge" from preservice training to both common and exceptional classroom situations should be observable. Through experience and awareness, teachers are able to improvise. Flexibility and adaptability are sometimes more desirable than a well-written lesson plan, because classrooms are dynamic. Novice teachers often hesitate to deviate from a plan, but effective teachers can do it with ease, capitalizing on a teachable moment or accommodating a schedule change. The ability to improvise is a characteristic more common to experienced educators than to beginners.

Research supports the following findings related to teacher experience:

• Teachers with more experience tend to show better planning skills, including a more hierarchical and organized structure in the presentation of their material (Borko & Livingston, 1989; Covino & Iwanicki, 1996; Jay, 2002; Yildirim, 2001).

• Effective experienced teachers are better able to apply a range of teaching strategies, and they demonstrate more depth and differentiation in learning activities (Covino & Iwanicki, 1996).

• Experienced teachers tend to know and understand their students' learning needs, learning styles, prerequisite skills, and interests better than beginners do (Borko & Livingston, 1989; Covino & Iwanicki, 1996; Jay, 2002).

• The classrooms of more experienced teachers are better organized around routines and plans for handling problems than are those of novices (Covino & Iwanicki, 1996; Cruickshank & Haefele, 2001).

• Teachers with more than three years of experience are more effective than those with three years or fewer (Nye, Konstantopoulos, & Hedges, 2004), but these differences seem to level off after five to eight years (Darling-Hammond, 2000; Scherer, 2001).

• Teacher expertise as defined by experience (as well as education and scores on licensing exams) accounts for as much as 40 percent of the variation in student achievement, which is more than race and socioeconomic status (Ferguson, 1991; Virshup, 1997).

• Schools with more beginning teachers tend to have lower student achievement (Betts, Rueben, & Danenberg, 2000; Fetler, 1999; Goe, 2002), and schools with student performance in the lowest quartile have more inexperienced teachers than those schools with student performance in the highest quartile (Esch et al., 2005).

Related Resources: Betts, Rueben, & Danenberg, 2000; Borko & Livingston, 1989; Covino & Iwanicki, 1996; Cruickshank & Haefele, 2001; Darling-Hammond, 2000; Education Review Office, 1998; Esch et al., 2005; Fetler, 1999; Goe, 2002; Haycock, 2000, 2003; Jay, 2002; Kerrins & Cushing, 1998; Neilsen, 1999; Nye et al., 2004; Scherer, 2001; Tell, 2001; Virshup, 1997; Yildirim, 2001.

Teachers of At-Risk Students: Prerequisites of Teacher Effectiveness

The research and literature related to effective teachers of at-risk students tend to focus on the teacher quality characteristics that are lacking in schools that serve a high number of poor and minority students. For example, poor and minority students are more likely than students in other school settings to have teachers who are teaching out of their fields, who are not certified to teach, who have little to no experience, or who perform more poorly on tests of verbal ability. One study found that in schools with a high percentage of minority students, 29 percent of secondary core-subject courses are taught by a teacher without at least a minor in the subject, versus 21 percent in schools with a lower percentage of minority students. The picture is even bleaker in high-poverty schools. In schools with a high percentage of poor students, 34 percent of secondary core-subject courses are taught by a teacher without at least a minor in the subject, versus 15 percent in schools with a low percentage of low-income students (Barton, 2003). Mathematics and science courses are more often taught to at-risk high school students by teachers without certification or a major in those areas than are other courses. (National Center for Education Statistics, 2000).

Recruiting teachers—and retaining them—is a significant challenge for urban districts with high numbers of poor and minority students. A study of New York state teachers found that teachers are more likely to take positions close to home or in areas that resemble their hometown. As a result, urban districts typically must import more teachers from urban areas than are available, resulting in a decreased pool of qualified teachers from which to draw (Boyd, Lankford, Loeb, & Wycoff, 2005). Similarly, a study in North Carolina found that vacancies at low-performing schools were more likely to be filled from outside the school district and by novice teachers (Clotfelter, Ladd, Vigdor, & Diaz, 2004).

Teacher training in appropriate methodologies is another correlate to student achievement. Unfortunately, poor and minority students are more likely to have a teacher who has not completed all teacher preparation requirements and therefore is not certified. Educational coursework—either through a teacher preparation program or extended through professional development—provides additional training needed to meet the needs of students. Kozol's (2005) exposé of the inequalities prevalent in the U.S. public education system illuminates this issue.

Teachers of poor and minority students are also more likely to be inexperienced than are their peers in high-income schools. In fact, one study found that in high-minority schools, 21 percent of teachers have three or fewer years of experience versus 10 percent in low-minority schools. The statistics for low-income schools are much the same: 20 percent of teachers in schools of low socioeconomic status (SES) have three or fewer years of experience versus 11 percent in higher-income schools (Barton, 2003). Similarly, a study of 11 North Carolina school districts revealed that black 7th grade students were more likely to have inexperienced teachers in mathematics and English than were white 7th grade students (Clotfelter, Ladd, & Vigdor, 2005).

As discussed earlier in this chapter, a direct relationship between teachers' verbal ability and student achievement has been well established. As for students at risk of failing, findings suggest that a higher percentage of teachers in schools with high percentages of minority and poor students have performed less well on tests of verbal ability; consequently, some of these teachers took remedial courses in reading and writing.

For children at risk, either through school factors or societal factors, some essential elements of a quality teacher are in short supply. Although there are many, many capable and committed teachers in challenging schools, the following findings demonstrate the gap between what we know about teacher quality and the teachers of poor and minority students:

• Effective teachers of at-risk students know their subject content and are able to communicate subject matter to students (Ilmer, Snyder, Erbaugh, & Kurtz, 1997; Lewis, 2001; National Academy of Sciences, 2004; Peart & Campbell, 1999).

• Teacher training about the use of a variety of materials to meet students' learning needs was a significant factor in reading-achievement gains of minority students (Armor et al., 1976).

• New teachers in schools with high-poverty levels scored in the lowest quartile of the SAT and ACT of all graduates from the Baccalaureate and Beyond Longitudinal Study (Shen, Mansberger, & Yang, 2004).

• Poor and minority students are more likely to have teachers who have emergency certification credentials (i.e., teacher who lack credentials for full certification) (Darling-Hammond, 1996; Esch, Chang-Ross, Tiffany-Morales,

& Shields, 2004; Kain & Singleton, 1996; National Center for Education Statistics, 2000).

• The number of remedial courses taken by teachers in the areas of mathematics, reading, and writing is inversely associated with the academic levels of students in high-poverty schools (Shen et al., 2004).

• The higher the teacher turnover in a school, the poorer the academic achievement of students (U.S. Department of Education, 2004).

Related Resources: Armor et al., 1976; Barton, 2003; Boyd et al., 2005; Clotfelter et al., 2005; Clotfelter et al., 2004; Darling-Hammond, 1996; Esch et al., 2004; Ilmer et al., 1997; Kain & Singleton, 1996, cited in Haycock, 2003; Lewis, 2001; National Center for Education Statistics, 2000; Peart & Campbell, 1999; Shen et al., 2004; U.S. Department of Education, 2004.

Teachers of High-Ability Students: Prerequisites of Teacher Effectiveness

Research and literature on effective teachers of gifted students mirrors that of the more general research on teacher quality. Thus, findings related to prerequisites for teaching high-ability students are similar to those discussed previously in the chapter. For example, effective teachers of gifted students tend to demonstrate strong communication skills and perform well on tests of verbal ability. They are valued by students for having high intelligence and intellectual curiosity similar to those of high-ability learners; however, certain aspects of the background and preparation of teachers of gifted and talented students warrant further discussion.

Effective teachers of gifted students are characterized as having in-depth subject-matter knowledge as well as in-depth knowledge of gifted education. This knowledge of gifted education includes an understanding of the characteristics of gifted learners, the needs of gifted learners, and effective approaches to instruction for gifted learners. Effective teachers of gifted and talented students are aware of their emotional and social needs as well as their academic needs.

Various studies support the finding that effective teachers of gifted students have taken coursework in gifted education and are certified to teach gifted students, if their state has such a certification. Training in gifted education is paramount to teacher effectiveness (Hunt & Seney, 2001; Seeley,

1989), both to provide teachers with foundational skills and understandings and to dispel myths about gifted students and appropriate gifted services (Colangelo, Assouline, & Gross, 2004; Copenhaver & McIntyre, 1992; Feldhusen, 1997). Leading researchers in gifted education recommended that a teacher of gifted students have at least 12 credits in gifted education (VanTassel-Baska & Little, 2003). Moreover, teachers of gifted students who have experience in teaching high-ability learners are better able to handle the demands that gifted learners place on their teachers. The following conclusions can be drawn from the research connecting effective teachers and high-ability students:

• Effective teachers of gifted students earned higher scores on tests of verbal ability than did the general population of teachers (Agne, 2001; Dubner, 1979; Silverman, 1995; VanTassel-Baska, 1993).

• Effective teachers of gifted students know the needs and characteristics of gifted learners and have received training in appropriate instructional teaching methods (Hansen & Feldhusen, 1994; Lee-Corbin & Denicolo, 1998; Sternberg & Grigorenko, 2002; Vaille & Quigley, 2002).

• Those teachers with more experience in teaching gifted students and with more coursework in gifted education are more adept at handling the diverse needs of gifted learners (Agne, 2001; Heath, 1997; Rash & Miller, 2000).

• Teachers of gifted students identified knowledge of gifted students and knowledge of subject matter as essential competencies of teachers who teach these students (Nelson & Prindle, 1992; Worley, 2006).

• Teachers in schools identified as providing strong differentiated experiences for high-ability students reported participation in and application of extensive professional development experiences related to the specific instructional needs of these students (Westberg & Archambault, 1997).

• Teachers trained in teaching gifted students used more varied learning experiences, were more energetic and enthusiastic, focused on more in-depth analysis in class discussions, and had more positive classroom environments than did untrained teachers (Feldhusen, 1991; Hansen & Feldhusen, 1994).

• Teacher experience correlated positively with the implementation of a variety of appropriate instructional methods in working with high-ability students (Rash & Miller, 2000), and level of experience also related to breadth in identifying common characteristics of gifted students (Copenhaver & McIntyre, 1992).

• Both experts in the field of gifted education and gifted students themselves have identified strong communication skills, intellectual curiosity, and high intelligence as characteristics of effective teachers of gifted students (Feldhusen, 1997; Heath, 1997; Maker, 1975; Nikakis, 2002; Vaille & Quigley, 2002).

Related Resources: Agne, 2001; Colangelo et al., 2004; Copenhaver & McIntyre, 1992; Dubner, 1979; Feldhusen, 1991, 1997; Hansen & Feldhusen, 1994; Heath, 1997; Hunt & Seney, 2001; Lee-Corbin & Denicolo, 1998; Maker, 1975; Nelson & Prindle, 1992; Nikakis, 2002; Rash & Miller, 2000; Seeley, 1989; Silverman, 1995; Sternberg & Grigorenko, 2002; Vaille & Quigley, 2002; VanTassel-Baska, 1993; VanTassel-Baska & Little, 2003; Westberg & Archambault, 1997; Worley, 2006.

Figure 1.1
Key References for Prerequisites for Effective Teaching

Reference	Verbal Ability	Knowledge of Teaching and Learning	Certification Status	Content Knowledge	Teaching Experience	Teachers of At-Risk Students	Teachers of High-Ability Students
Agne, 2001	•				•		•
Armor et al., 1976		•			•	•	
Ashton & Crocker, 1987		•					
Barton, 2003			•	•	•	•	
Berliner, 1986				•			
Betts et al., 2000					•		
Blair, 2000		•					
Borko & Livingston, 1989					•		
Brookhart & Loadman, 1992				•			
Carlsen, 1987				•			
Carlsen & Wilson, 1988				•			
Colangelo et al., 2004		•					•
Copenhaver & McIntyre, 1992					•		•
Covino & Iwanicki, 1996				•	•		
Cruickshank & Haefele, 2001					•		
Darling-Hammond, 1996			•	•		•	
Darling-Hammond, 2000			•	•			
Darling-Hammond, 2001	•	•	•	•	•		
Darling-Hammond et al., 2001			•	•			
Darling-Hammond et al., 2005			•				
Darling-Hammond & Sykes, 2003		•					
Dozier & Bertotti, 2000			•				
Druva & Anderson, 1983		•		•			
Dubner, 1979	•						•
Education Review Office, 1998					•		
Esch et al., 2004			•			•	
Feldhusen, 1991		•					•

Figure 1.1 *Continued*
Key References for Prerequisites for Effective Teaching

Reference	Verbal Ability	Knowledge of Teaching and Learning	Certification Status	Content Knowledge	Teaching Experience	Teachers of At-Risk Students	Teachers of High-Ability Students
Feldhusen, 1997	•	•					•
Ferguson & Womack, 1993		•	•	•			
Fetler, 1999		•	•	•	•		
Goe, 2002					•		
Goldhaber & Brewer, 2000			•	•			
Hansen & Feldhusen, 1994		•					•
Hanushek, 1971	•	•					
Hawk et al., 1985			•				
Haycock, 2000	•				•		
Haycock, 2003			•			•	
Heath, 1997	•				•		•
Hill et al., 2005		•		•			
Holt-Reynolds, 1999		•		•			
Ilmer et al., 1997	•			•		•	
Ingersoll, 2001			•				
Jay, 2002					•		
Johnson, 1997				•			
Johnson et al., 2005		•					
Kerrins & Cushing, 1998					•		
Laczko-Kerr & Berliner, 2002			•				
Lee-Corbin & Denicolo, 1998		•					•
Lewis, 2001	•			•		•	
Lilly, 1992			•				
Mason et al., 1992		•					
Mathews, 1999		•	•				
Miller et al., 1998		•	•				
Mitchell, 1998				•			

Figure 1.1 *Continued*
Key References for Prerequisites for Effective Teaching

Reference	Verbal Ability	Knowledge of Teaching and Learning	Certification Status	Content Knowledge	Teaching Experience	Teachers of At-Risk Students	Teachers of High-Ability Students
Monk & King, 1994		•		•			
Murnane, 1985	•						
National Association of Secondary School Principals, 1997				•			
National Board for Professional Teaching Standards, n.d.				•			
NCES, 1992	•						
NCES, 2000			•			•	
Neilsen, 1999					•		
Nelson & Prindle, 1992		•		•			•
Nikakis, 2002	•						•
Nye et al., 2004					•		
Peart & Campbell, 1999				•		•	
Qu & Becker, 2003			•				
Rash & Miller, 2000					•		•
Rowan et al., 1997	•			•			
Schalock et al., 1998		•					
Scherer, 2001		•	•		•		
Shellard & Protheroe, 2000		•		•			
Shen et al., 2004	•					•	
Shulman, 1987				•			
Silverman, 1995	•						•
Southern Regional Education Board, 1999		•					
Sternberg & Grigorenko, 2002		•					•
Strauss & Sawyer, 1986			•				
Tell, 2001		•					
Thomas B. Fordham Foundation, 1999	•	•					

Figure 1.1 *Continued*
Key References for Prerequisites for Effective Teaching

Reference	Verbal Ability	Knowledge of Teaching and Learning	Certification Status	Content Knowledge	Teaching Experience	Teachers of At-Risk Students	Teachers of High-Ability Students
Traina, 1999				•			
U.S. Department of Education, 2004					•		
Vaille & Quigley, 2002		•	•				•
VanTassel-Baska, 1993	•						•
Virshup, 1997					•		
Wenglinsky, 2000	•	•		•			
Wenglinsky, 2002		•		•			
Westberg & Archambault, 1997		•					•
Wilson et al., 2001				•			
Wise, 2000		•	•				
Yildirim, 2001					•		

2

The Teacher as a Person

Esperanza teaches a diverse group of students. English language learners, at-risk students, honors students, and everyone else find their seats in her classroom for 90 minutes of science instruction. Spend just two minutes listening to students coming into the class and you will hear her ask a student about a sibling or compliment another student's performance in a sporting event. You can see Esperanza circulating around the room smiling, leaning over to check work, and nodding an acknowledgment to a student arriving late. As students finish their warm-up activity, the instruction begins and the interplay between students and their teacher continues. She knows her students and freely admits that they can be a tough bunch, but she loves each and every one of them. Esperanza is aptly named, for she offers hope to students every day as she lives out her ethic of caring.

Much of the recent research on teacher effectiveness focuses on relating teacher behaviors to student achievement. Quite a bit of the research, however, has delved into stakeholders' perceptions of good teaching—what students, administrators, and teachers themselves think makes an effective teacher. Studies suggest that instructional and management processes are keys to effectiveness, but many interview and survey responses about effective teaching emphasize the teacher's affective characteristics, or social and emotional behaviors, more than pedagogical practice. These affective characteristics are difficult to quantify; however, characteristics such as a love of children, a love of work, and positive relationships with colleagues and with children contribute to a teacher's feeling of happiness. Noddings (2005) explained that a teacher's happiness can affect the classroom climate and therefore affect students. Moreover, the teacher's psychological influence on students has been linked to student achievement in various effectiveness studies. This chapter explores what we know about teachers' affective characteristics as they relate to effectiveness and to perceptions of effectiveness. Figure 2.1, at the end of the chapter, lists the major characteristics, along with key references for additional reading.

The Role of Caring

Effective teachers care about their students and demonstrate that they care in such a way that their students are aware of it, as we see in the classroom example at the beginning of this chapter. Several studies exploring what makes a good teacher show the importance of caring in the eyes of teachers and students. Also, supervisors who rate teachers place priority on how teachers show students that they are caring and supportive.

Caring is a broad term, perhaps as broad as effectiveness itself. One study defines caring as an act of bringing out the best in students through affirmation and encouragement. Obviously, the characteristics of caring go well beyond knowing the students, including qualities such as patience, trust, honesty, and courage. Specific teacher attributes that show caring include listening, gentleness, understanding, knowledge of students as individuals, nurturing, warmth and encouragement, and an overall love for children.

Listening

Effective teachers practice focused and sympathetic listening to show students they care about not only what happens in the classroom but about students' lives in general. These teachers initiate two-way communication that exudes trust, tact, honesty, humility, and care. In the act of listening, these teachers actually pay attention to and understand what the students say. They are dedicated to bettering student lives, and they demonstrate their understanding through tenderness, patience, and gentleness. Moreover, research indicates that children want to be nurtured and that they value teachers who are kind, gentle, and encouraging. Particularly for elementary students, gentleness in a teacher is a sign of caring and an important element in perceived effectiveness. Think of a child who leaves the care of a mother or a nurturing caretaker and enters the kindergarten classroom, only to find that he or she is one of 20 students to whom the teacher must attend. The environment is new, important people in the child's life are new, and he or she is most likely overwhelmed. While the teacher may not be able to replace a mother's love or the comforts of familiar surroundings, the teacher can help the child in the transition by making the student feel important and cared about.

Understanding

Students highly value teachers' understanding of their concerns and questions. Interviews with students consistently reveal that students want teachers who listen to their arguments and assist them in working out their problems. They want teachers who hold them in mutual respect and who are willing to talk about their own personal lives and experiences. Through appropriate self-disclosure, teachers become human in the eyes of students. Being available to students and showing a deep understanding of students legitimizes the teacher as a person when he or she demonstrates genuine concern and empathy toward students.

Knowing Students

Effective, caring teachers know students both formally and informally. They use every opportunity at school and in the community to keep the lines of communication open. Many educational stakeholders emphasize that effective teachers know their students individually, not only understanding each student's learning style and needs but also understanding the student's personality, likes and dislikes, and personal situations that may affect behavior and performance in school. Effective teachers care for students first as people, and second as students. They respect each student as an individual.

Research on caring teachers yields the following important points:

• Caring teachers who know their students create relationships that enhance the learning process (Peart & Campbell, 1999).

• Effective teachers consistently emphasize their love for children as one key element of their success (Brophy & Good, 1986).

• Teachers who create a supportive and warm classroom climate tend to be more effective with all students (Peart & Campbell, 1999).

• Caring teachers are intentionally aware of student cultures outside the school (Ilmer et al., 1997).

• Caring teachers truly believe that each student has a right to a caring and competent teacher (Collinson, Killeavy, & Stephenson, 1999).

• Caring teachers appropriately respect confidentiality issues when dealing with students (Collinson et al., 1999).

• Caring teachers value care and learning as important qualities for educating students to their full potential (Collinson et al., 1999).

• Students who perceive their teachers as caring exert academic effort and social responsibility (Wentzel, 1997).

• Teachers in effective schools go beyond a mere respectful relationship to a caring relationship with students (Langer, 2000).

Related Resources: Bain & Jacobs, 1990; Brophy & Good, 1986; Collinson et al.,1999; Cotton, 1999, 2000; Cruickshank & Haefele, 2001; Emmer, Evertson, & Anderson, 1980; Good & Brophy, 1997; Ilmer et al., 1997; Johnson, 1997; Langer, 2000; NASSP, 1997; Peart & Campbell, 1999; Thomas & Montgomery, 1998; Wang, Haertel, & Walberg, 1993a, 1993b; Wentzel, 1997; Yamaguchi, Strawser, & Higgins, 1997.

The Role of Fairness and Respect

Beyond a demonstration of caring, an effective teacher establishes a rapport and credibility with students by emphasizing, modeling, and practicing fairness and respect. Respect and equity are identified as the prerequisites of effective teaching in the eyes of students. In fact, students interviewed for their views on effective teachers consistently note the importance of fairness and respect at all levels of schooling—from elementary through high school.

The elements of fairness and respect are highlighted in many studies. Students stated that effective teachers respond to misbehavior at an individual level rather than holding a whole class responsible for the actions of one student or a small group of students. They know and understand the facts before responding to any disciplinary situation, and then tell students specifically what they did wrong. Moreover, they tell students what they need to do right. Furthermore, students expect teachers to treat them equitably—when they behave as well as when they misbehave—and to avoid demonstrations of favoritism.

Effective teachers continually demonstrate respect and understanding, along with fairness regarding race, cultural background, and gender. Students' perceptions of teacher effectiveness emphasize racial impartiality, with equitable treatment of all students. The students expect teachers not to allow ethnicity to affect their treatment or expectations of students.

Interviews and surveys of perceptions of fairness in the classroom indicate the following key points:

• Students associate respect with fairness and expect teachers to treat them as people (Agne, 1992; Covino & Iwanicki, 1996; Thomas & Montgomery, 1998).

• Students perceive effective teachers as those who avoid using ridicule and who prevent situations in which students lose respect in front of their peers (NASSP, 1997).

• Effective teachers practice gender, racial, and ethnic fairness (Peart & Campbell, 1999).

• Students associate fairness and respect with a teacher being consistent and providing opportunities for students to have input into the classroom (Emmer et al., 1980).

Related Resources: Agne, 1992; Collinson et al., 1999; Cotton, 1999, 2000; Emmer et al., 1980; Good & Brophy, 1997; McBer, 2000; NASSP, 1997; Peart & Campbell, 1999; Thomas & Montgomery, 1998; Yamaguchi et al., 1997.

Social Interactions with Students

Teachers and students spend much of their day interacting academically; however, social interactions and those that give the teacher opportunities to demonstrate caring, fairness, and respect have been shown to be an important element of teacher effectiveness. A teacher's ability to relate to students and to make positive, caring connections with them plays a significant role in cultivating a positive learning environment and promoting student achievement.

Effective teachers use a wide variety of strategies to interact with students. However, the basis for these interactions goes beyond the four walls of the classroom. In fact, students revealed that effective teachers demonstrate interest in students' lives beyond the classroom. Teachers who attend sporting events, concerts, and other special programs in which their students participate are valued by their students. Additionally, researchers contend that constructive social interactions between teachers and students not only contribute to student learning and achievement, but also increase student self-esteem by fostering feelings of belonging to the classroom and the school.

Teachers who are aware of their own style of interacting with their students are able to provide a more favorable learning environment for all students. Through social interactions with students, effective teachers are able to individually, realistically, and successfully challenge each and every student to succeed.

Aspects of effective teaching related to social interaction involve the following:

• Effective teachers consistently behave in a friendly and personal manner while maintaining appropriate teacher-student role structure (Brookhart & Loadman, 1992; Peart & Campbell, 1999).

• Effective teachers work *with* students as opposed to doing things *to* or *for* them (Kohn, 1996).

• Productive interactions involve giving students responsibility and respect, and also treating secondary students as adults when appropriate (NASSP, 1997).

• Teachers who are considered effective allow students to participate in decision making (Education USA Special Report, n.d.; Kohn, 1996).

• Effective teachers pay attention to what students have to say (Peart & Campbell, 1999; Thomas & Montgomery, 1998).

• Students indicate that effective teachers spend more time interacting and working directly with them than ineffective teachers (NASSP, 1997; Peart & Campbell, 1999).

• Effective teachers have a good sense of humor and are willing to share jokes (NASSP, 1997; Peart & Campbell, 1999).

Related Resources: Bain & Jacobs, 1990; Bloom, 1984; Brookhart & Loadman, 1992; Collinson et al., 1999; Cotton, 1999, 2000; Cruickshank & Haefele, 2001; Darling-Hammond, 2001; Education USA Special Report, n.d.; Good & Brophy, 1997; Kohn, 1996; NASSP, 1997; Peart & Campbell, 1999; Porter & Brophy, 1988; Thomas & Montgomery, 1998; Wang et al., 1993a, 1993b; Yamaguchi et al., 1997.

Promoting Enthusiasm and Motivating Learning

The teachers' enthusiasm for teaching, learning, and their subject matter has been shown to be an important part of effective teaching, both in supporting positive relationships with students and in encouraging student achievement. Students say that teachers can effectively motivate them by encouraging them to be responsible for their own learning, maintaining an organized classroom environment, setting high standards, assigning appropriate challenges, and providing reinforcement and encouragement during tasks. These students see effective teachers as motivational leaders.

Research indicates that effective teachers have residual positive effects on their students' willingness to work to their potential and beyond. Consequently, less effective teachers may actually extinguish students' interest in the subject. Good teachers realize and address the fact that some students prefer to sit quietly on the sideline; however, they do not stop involving them.

By finding a way to motivate a student to learn, a teacher contributes to a student's evolving attitude toward a particular subject or activity. In other words, the teacher can bring out the best in that student. An effective teacher recognizes that students vary in their motivation levels. An effective teacher knows how to support intrinsically motivated students and seeks ways to provide extrinsic motivation to students who need it. Motivating students consists of making students receptive to and excited about learning, as well as making them aware of the importance and value of learning itself. By establishing positive attitudes and perceptions about learning, the effective teacher makes the learner feel comfortable in the classroom. As a particular example of establishing positive attitudes, teachers who provide mastery learning techniques for their students improve the attitudes of their students. They also increase academic self-concept, interest in the subject area, and the desire to learn more about the subject. Emphasizing higher-order mental processes along with mastering learning strategies tends to create a learning environment that is exciting and constantly new and playful.

Researchers have investigated the influence of teacher enthusiasm on student motivation and learning, with the following results and conclusions:

• High levels of motivation in teachers relate to high levels of achievement in students (Rowan et al., 1997).

• Teachers' enthusiasm for learning and for their subject matter has been shown to be an important factor in student motivation, which is closely linked to student achievement (Covino & Iwanicki, 1996; Monk & King, 1994).

• Some studies indicate that the enthusiasm factor is more significant with older students than younger ones, but effective primary teachers also demonstrate enthusiasm for their work as part of their overall effectiveness (Bain & Jacobs, 1990).

Related Resources: Bain & Jacobs, 1990; Belton, 1996; Bloom, 1984; Brophy & Good, 1986; Collinson et al., 1999; Covino & Iwanicki, 1996; Darling-Hammond, 2000; Johnson, 1997; Monk & King, 1994; Palmer, 1990; Peart & Campbell, 1999; Rowan et al., 1997; Wang et al., 1993a, 1993b.

A Teacher's Attitude Toward the Teaching Profession

An important facet of professionalism and of effectiveness in the classroom is a teacher's dedication to students and to the job of teaching. Through examining several sources of evidence, a dual commitment to student learning and to personal learning has been found repeatedly in effective teachers. A common belief among effective teachers, which reveals their dual commitment, is that it is up to them to provide a multitude of tactics to reach students. In essence, effective teachers view themselves as responsible for the success of their students.

The effective teacher truly believes that all students can learn—it is not just a slogan. These teachers also believe that they must know their students, their subject, and themselves, while continuing to account for the fact that students learn differently. Through differentiation of instruction, effective teachers reach their students, and together they enjoy their successes.

Effective teachers also work collaboratively with other staff members. They are willing to share their ideas and assist other teachers with difficulties. Collaborative environments create positive working relationships and help retain teachers. Additionally, effective teachers volunteer to lead work teams and to be mentors to new teachers. Effective teachers are informal leaders on the cutting edge of reform and are not afraid to take risks to improve education for all students. These informal leaders are the ones administrators typically call on for opinions and for help in effecting change. One study found teachers with National Board Certification to be effective advocates for education in their communities, districts, and schools (Mitchell, 1998).

Effective teachers invest in their own education. They model to their students that education and learning are valuable by taking classes and participating in professional development, conferences, and inservice training. Additionally, they discuss their participation in these activities with students in a positive manner. Effective teachers learn and grow as they expect their students to learn and grow. They serve as powerful examples of lifelong learners as they find ways to develop professionally.

The relationship between teachers' attitudes and effectiveness can be summarized in the following ways:

• Effective teachers exude positive attitudes about life and teaching (Mitchell, 1998).

• Effective teachers believe that extra hours spent preparing and reflecting upon instruction are well worth the student outcomes—specifically with regard to student achievement (Bratton, 1998).

• Promoting and participating in a collegial, collaborative work environment results in more positive attitudes in teachers (Southeast Center for Teaching Quality [SECTQ], 2003).

• Effective teachers do not make excuses for student outcomes; they hold their students responsible while also accepting responsibility themselves (Allington, 2002).

• Effective teachers believe that their students can learn and that they can help students learn (SECTQ, 2003).

Related Resources: Allington, 2002; Bain & Jacobs, 1990; Blair, 2000; Brookhart & Loadman, 1992; Cawelti, 1999; Covino & Iwanicki, 1996; McBer, 2000; Mitchell, 1998; National Board for Professional Teaching Standards (NBPTS), n.d.; Porter & Brophy, 1988; Rowan et al., 1997; SECTQ, 2003; Thomas & Montgomery, 1998; Virshup, 1997; Wong & Wong, 1998.

The Role of Reflective Practice

Another element of professionalism often cited as part of effective teaching is a teacher's reflective practice, or careful review of and thoughtfulness about one's own teaching process. The role of reflection has been described repeatedly in studies of teacher effectiveness. Those studies include interviews and surveys of teachers judged effective according to their students' achievement rates, studies of teachers certified under the National Board of Professional Teaching Standards, and case studies of effective schools. Effective teachers continually practice self-evaluation and self-critique as learning tools. Reflective teachers portray themselves as students of learning. They are curious about the art and science of teaching and about themselves as effective teachers. They constantly improve lessons, think about how to reach particular children, and seek and try out new approaches in the classroom to better meet the needs of their learners.

Some researchers define reflective teachers as introspective. They seek a greater understanding of teaching through scholarly study and professional reading. Through reflective practice, effective teachers monitor their teaching because they want to be better teachers and to make a difference in the lives of students.

Effective teachers invite feedback by eliciting information and criticism from others. Additionally, in the interest of improving their ability to have a positive impact on student learning, these teachers readily accept constructive criticism and reflect upon it. Reflective practice can initially result in confusion for the teacher; the process requires open-mindedness, honesty, and sufficient time to change teaching behaviors.

Thoughtful questions generated by research can guide teachers in reflecting on practice. Effective teachers realize that reflective practices are more than simply preservice or inservice exercises. Indeed, reflective practices are crucial to lifelong learning and a professional necessity.

Thoughtful reflection translates into enhanced teacher efficacy, and a teacher's sense of efficacy has an impact on how he or she approaches instructional content and students. While efficacy does change for teachers as they encounter new experiences, such as the use of new materials or teaching at different grade levels, they are more likely to have additional positive experiences as they reflect on these new experiences. Educators' confidence in their ability to facilitate students' learning and understanding of material is observable by others. In particular, when teachers are confident, they communicate the belief of their own efficacy to students.

Additional findings on the value of reflective practices include the following:

• Teachers rate analyzing and seeking to improve their own teaching as an important factor in their teaching effectiveness (Covino & Iwanicki, 1996).

• Effective teachers may reflect on their work formally or informally; for example, they may review a day's work mentally, keep a journal or portfolio, meet regularly with a mentor or with colleagues, or assess a videotaped recording of their teaching (Good & Brophy, 1997; NBPTS, n.d.). Regardless of the mode, the key is reflection.

• Teachers whose students have high achievement rates continually mention reflection on their work as an important part of improving their teaching (Mitchell, 1998).

• Belief in one's efficacy and maintaining high expectations for students are common among teachers who reflect (NBPTS, n.d.).

Related Resources: Collinson et al., 1999; Covino & Iwanicki, 1996; Cruickshank & Haefele, 2001; Demmon-Berger, 1986; Good & Brophy, 1997; Mitchell, 1998; NBPTS, n.d.; Thomas & Montgomery, 1998.

Teachers of At-Risk Students: The Teacher as a Person

Effective teachers of at-risk students share many of the characteristics of those already discussed; however, one of the most cited characteristics in the literature is the caring teacher. Indeed, a hallmark of caring teachers is that they seek to understand the needs, hopes, and aspirations of their students. They know students on an individual basis and demonstrate their concern for both the educational success and personal needs of their students. More-over, they get to know the students' families and their communities. This level of commitment and caring about the educational needs and personal well-being of their students is important for all teachers, but appears to be especially so for teachers of children with special needs (Boyle-Baise, 2005; Hamre & Pianta, 2005).

Demonstrating care for students takes on many forms, both in a personal and an academic sense. Consistent with their primary role as teachers, effec-tive teachers care about their students' academic well-being and seek to help all students succeed, including at-risk students. They hold high expectations for their students and provide support for reaching those expectations by motivating students to learn and providing encouragement. Teachers of at-risk students, however, do not merely sit on the sidelines and cheer. Rather, they are willing to help students by staying after school or coming in early to provide assistance. They help their students set goals, and they provide the necessary support to achieve those goals.

In a personal sense, caring teachers of at-risk students have been described as compassionate, tolerant, open-minded, motivating, nurturing, firm, and dedicated. They use humor to diffuse difficult situations, and they are caring yet firm. One author described effective teachers of at-risk students as "warm demanders" (Howard, 2002). In other words, their students know the teach-ers care deeply for them yet also know that they are expected to learn. These teachers work to ensure that students attend school on a regular basis. And, perhaps most important, these teachers see their students as individuals, not as "poor" students or "minority" students.

Teacher efficacy is a critical characteristic of teachers of at-risk students. In particular, effective teachers do not allow the background characteristics of their students to cloud their belief in their students' ability to achieve aca-demically. Factors affecting student achievement such as poverty, parent participation in schooling, nutrition, and a host of others are viewed as obstacles to overcome, not obstacles that are insurmountable. Effective teachers believe that "they could 'get through' even to children with shaky motivation or home background" (Armor et al., 1976, p. 49). A study of the effects of teacher efficacy revealed that the teachers' belief that they could make a difference in the lives of their students had a stronger impact on low-achieving students than it did on high-achieving students (Midgley, Feldlaufer, & Eccles, 1989). A summary of the research on these types of student-teacher interactions appears below:

• Teachers, student teachers, and higher education faculty identify knowledge of students' community and culture, awareness of the teachers' own biases and prejudices, and ability to motivate students to learn as critical characteristics of effective teachers of at-risk students (Ilmer et al., 1997; Zeichner, 2003).

• Effective teachers get to know students on an individual basis and are willing to help students achieve (Corbett & Wilson, 2002).

• Effective teachers of at-risk students are caring and dedicated, know students well, and work with them to achieve goals by staying after school or coming in on Saturdays (Baker, 1999; Bernard, 2003; Pressley, Raphael, Gallagher, & DiBella, 2004).

• In a study of unsafe schools, teachers identified by students as most effective in dealing with violent situations were described as caring about the students, knowing the students' parents and the community, and being willing to intervene (Astor, Meyer, & Behre, 1999).

• Students of teachers who encourage them to succeed put forth more effort than students of those teachers who are not encouraging (Ferguson, 2002).

• Positive relationships among teachers and at-risk students lead to better class conduct and better standardized test scores (McDermott & Rothenberg, 1999; Sanders & Jordan, 2000).

• At-risk students whose teachers exhibited excitement and enthusiasm in teaching and who positively interacted with students performed as well as their peers who are not at risk (Hamre & Pianta, 2005).

Related Resources: Adams & Singh, 1998; Armor et al., 1976; Astor et al., 1999; Baker, 1999; Boyle-Baise, 2005; Corbett & Wilson, 2002; Ferguson, 2002; Hamre & Pianta, 2005;

Howard, 2002; Ilmer et al., 1997; McDermott & Rothenberg, 1999; Midgley et al., 1989; Pressley et al., 2004; Sanders & Jordan, 2000; Zeichner, 2003.

Teachers of High-Ability Students: The Teacher as a Person

Much of what we know about the teacher as a person we know from the students themselves. In one survey, gifted students indicated that they valued the personal and social characteristics of a teacher more than the teacher's cognitive and classroom management abilities (Maddux, Samples-Lachman, & Cummings, 1985). They value teachers who are friendly, have confidence, and have a good sense of humor. A review of literature revealed that in addition to these traits, effective teachers of gifted students are willing to work hard and devote the time necessary to do so (Feldhusen, VanTassel-Baska, & Seeley, 1989). Others describe effective teachers of gifted and talented students as passionate about their own learning and the learning of their students (Vaille & Quigley, 2002). Teachers of gifted students experience a heightened sense of self-efficacy when they have confidence in their knowledge of content and pedagogy as well as in themselves (Hutchinson, 2004).

As with other students, gifted students clearly value personal relationships with their teachers. Teachers who get to know students on an individual basis are perceived by their students as concerned about their educational and personal well-being. Multiple studies revealed that the most memorable teachers for gifted students were those with whom they had developed a personal relationship based on mutual respect (see, for example, Bloom, 1985; Carper, 2002). This personal, caring relationship is related not only to providing academic support and holding high expectations, but also to the teachers' intellectual characteristics as perceived by the student. In fact, there is some evidence that gifted students tend to reject teachers who do not care for the subjects they teach, who lack intellectual curiosity, and who do not exhibit enthusiasm for the teaching profession (Bloom, 1985; Csikszentmihalyi et al., 1993). Furthermore, recommendations and identified competencies for teachers of the gifted generally include an emphasis on skill in counseling gifted students, both in terms of academic and career counseling and in terms of supporting the special social and emotional needs of the students (Nelson & Prindle, 1992; Shore & Delcourt, 1996). Research findings related to teachers of high-ability learners include the following:

• Memorable teachers of gifted students model an interest in teaching and in their professional lives through enthusiasm for their subject (Csikszentmihalyi et al., 1993; Quek, 2005; Whitlock & Ducette, 1989).

• Gifted students value teachers with whom they have a personal, caring relationship (Bloom, 1985; Carper, 2002; Csikszentmihalyi et al., 1993; Heath, 1997; Nikakis, 2002; Quek, 2005).

• Effective teachers of gifted students recognize a wide range of characteristics that are common in gifted students, and they are aware of and responsive to the individual differences that emerge based on diversity of background, talent, and special needs (Copenhaver & McIntyre, 1992; Eyre et al., 2002; Ford & Trotman, 2001).

• Effective teachers of gifted students tend to take the talents of their students seriously (Csikszentmihalyi et al., 1993); therefore, students feel validated.

• Teachers who have high standards and expectations and are committed to supporting students' efforts and interests are most memorable to gifted students (Colangelo, Assouline, & Lupkowski-Shoplik, 2004; Cox, Daniel, & Boston, 1985; Whalen, 1998).

• Teachers of gifted students are characterized as being lifelong learners (Bernal, 1994; Emerick, 1992; Feldhusen, 1997).

• Effective teachers of gifted students exude enthusiasm through their positive outlook and through their own joy of learning (Hansen & Feldhusen, 1994; Quek, 2005; Worley, 2006).

• A teacher who has a personal sense of security and who reflects on teaching has a greater sense of self-efficacy in working with gifted students (Heath, 1997; Thomas & Montgomery, 1998; Westberg & Archambault, 1997).

Related Resources: Bernal, 1994; Bloom, 1985; Carper, 2002; Colangelo, Assouline, & Lupkowski- Shoplik, 2004; Copenhaver & McIntyre, 1992; Cox et al., 1985; Csikszentmihalyi et al., 1993; Emerick, 1992; Eyre et al., 2002; Feldhusen, 1997; Feldhusen et al., 1989; Ford & Trotman, 2001; Hansen & Feldhusen, 1994; Heath, 1997; Hutchinson, 2004; Maddux et al., 1985; Nelson & Prindle, 1992; Nikakis, 2002; Quek, 2005; Shore & Delcourt, 1996; Thomas & Montgomery, 1998; Vaille & Quigley, 2002; Westberg & Archambault, 1997; Whitlock & Ducette, 1989; Worley, 2006.

Figure 2.1
Key References for The Teacher as a Person

Reference	Caring	Fairness and Respect	Interactions with Students	Enthusiasm and Motivation	Attitude Toward Teaching	Reflective Practice	Teachers of At-Risk Students	Teachers of High-Ability Students
Armor et al., 1976					•	•	•	
Astor et al., 1999	•		•				•	
Bain & Jacobs, 1990	•		•	•	•			
Bernal, 1994					•			•
Blair, 2000					•			
Bloom, 1984	•		•	•				•
Boyle-Baise, 2005	•						•	
Brookhart & Loadman, 1992			•		•			
Brophy & Good, 1986	•			•				
Carper, 2002	•							•
Cawelti, 1999					•			
Colangelo, Assouline, & Lupkowski-Shoplik, 2004	•			•				•
Collinson et al., 1999	•	•	•	•		•		
Copenhaver & McIntyre, 1992			•					•
Corbett & Wilson, 2002			•				•	
Cotton, 1999	•	•	•					
Cotton, 2000	•	•	•					
Covino & Iwanicki, 1996				•	•	•		
Cox et al., 1985	•			•				•
Cruickshank & Haefele, 2001	•		•			•		
Csikszentmihalyi et al., 1993	•		•	•	•			•
Darling-Hammond, 2000				•				
Darling-Hammond, 2001			•					
Demmon-Berger, 1986						•		
Education USA Special Report, n.d.			•					

Figure 2.1 *Continued*
Key References for The Teacher as a Person

Reference	Caring	Fairness and Respect	Interactions with Students	Enthusiasm and Motivation	Attitude Toward Teaching	Reflective Practice	Teachers of At-Risk Students	Teachers of High-Ability Students
Emmer et al., 1980	•	•						
Feldhusen, 1997					•			•
Ford & Trotman, 2001			•					•
Good & Brophy, 1997	•	•	•			•		
Hamre & Pianta, 2005	•		•	•			•	
Hansen & Feldhusen, 1994					•			•
Howard, 2002	•						•	
Johnson, 1997	•		•	•				
Kohn, 1996			•					
McBer, 2000		•			•			
Midgley et al., 1989						•	•	
Mitchell, 1998					•	•		
Monk & King, 1994				•				
NASSP, 1997	•	•	•					
NBPTS, n.d.					•	•		
Noddings, 2005					•			
Palmer, 1990				•				
Peart & Campbell, 1999	•	•	•	•				
Porter & Brophy, 1988			•		•			
Pressley et al., 2004	•		•				•	
Rowan et al., 1997				•	•			
Thomas & Montgomery, 1998	•	•	•		•	•		
Vaille & Quigley, 2002				•				•
Virshup, 1997					•			
Wang et al., 1993a	•		•	•				
Wang et al., 1993b	•		•	•				

Figure 2.1 *Continued* **Key References for The Teacher as a Person**								
Reference	Caring	Fairness and Respect	Interactions with Students	Enthusiasm and Motivation	Attitude Toward Teaching	Reflective Practice	Teachers of At-Risk Students	Teachers of High-Ability Students
Westberg & Archambeault, 1997						•		•
Wong & Wong, 1998					•			
Yamaguchi et al., 1997	•	•	•					
Zeichner, 2003			•				•	

3

Classroom Management and Organization

The students walked in the door and picked up a pencil from the basket as they passed by it. On their way to their seats, the 3rd graders moved a magnet with their name on it to a section of the chalkboard labeled "Present." They put away their materials, took out paper, and began working on the opening task that was printed on the board. Matthew, a fifth-year teacher, moved around the room, inquired about missing homework, and wrote some notes during the first few minutes of class. When most of the students were done, the class went over the morning starter activity together. The signs of organization were every-where, right down to the effortless way that materials were distributed with just the mention of the word "baskets," which signaled six children to go and get baskets containing glue, crayons, and scissors for their fellow classmates.

An effective teacher plans and prepares for the organization of the class-room with the same care and precision used to design a high-quality lesson. Components of the organizational plan of a classroom include room arrangement, discipline, creating routines, and a plan to teach students how their learning environment is organized. To the extent possible, effec-tive teachers envision what is needed to make the classroom run smoothly. A key difference between beginning and experienced educators is that the novice tends to leap into the content the first week of school, while the senior teacher focuses on creating a positive classroom climate and then works aca-demics into that objective.

One survey of superintendents and principals indicated that a major chal-lenge faced by new teachers is their inability to maintain control in the class-room (Johnson, 2004). All teachers—novice and experienced alike—recognize the challenges of classroom management and understand that this aspect of quality teaching is vital (Sokal, Smith, & Mowat, 2003). Experienced teachers, however, understand the dividends paid by attending to classroom rules and procedures early on in the school year (Emmer, Evertson, & Worsham, 2003).

The effective teacher is not just someone who knows how to support student learning through instructional techniques, strong curricular materials, and rapport with the class. The effective teacher must create an overall environment conducive to learning. Orchestrating this supportive learning environment requires that a teacher practice skills in classroom organization and management. It also requires consistency in behavioral expectations and responses. The effective educator attends to these elements in a proactive way to establish a positive classroom climate oriented toward learning. Figure 3.1, at the end of this chapter, summarizes specific elements of the effective learning environment and links these elements to key references.

Using Classroom Management Skills

Successful classroom management involves much more than rules and discipline. Indeed, research into classroom management demonstrates that effective teachers are proactive about student behavior, and they involve students in the process of establishing and maintaining rules and routines. Doyle (1986) defined management as "the actions and strategies teachers use to solve the problem of order in classrooms" (p. 397), rather than responses to disciplinary situations. Effective teachers establish responses to common classroom issues of order that allow them to focus maximum time and energy on the instructional process. There is little time or inclination for students to misbehave when the classroom experience is engaging.

Effective classroom managers are thoroughly prepared and keep their students actively involved in the teaching and learning process. The primary ingredient here for teacher effectiveness is readiness. Effective teachers are prepared for students on a daily basis, from the very first day of school to the very last. Creating a productive classroom environment includes practical planning, such as developing functional floor plans with teacher and student work areas, wall spaces, and furniture placed within the classroom for optimal benefit.

Classroom managers who are prepared for the ups and downs of the instructional day work to create a setting that responds to the ebb and flow of the students. A positive attitude conveys this preparedness to students. This positive attitude is contagious; it spreads throughout the classroom.

Concerning the connection between classroom attitude and student achievement, a study in the Los Angeles Unified School District indicated that students whose teachers were positive, enthusiastic, and motivated performed better academically than students of those teachers who did not exhibit these characteristics (Fidler, 2002).

In addition to arranging the physical setting, effective teachers establish and actively teach rules and procedures at the beginning of the school year and rehearse them in the context in which they will be applied. They consistently and fairly enforce the rules for all students. Good classroom managers are effective monitors of students, as well. These teachers are keen observers of student behaviors and are adept at discerning and addressing potential disruptions. Over and over again, the term "with-it-ness," meaning awareness of surroundings, is used to describe teachers who are effective classroom managers. Moreover, effective teachers who are aware of student behaviors have a tendency to be near problems when they erupt, and so they can quell them quickly.

Many studies show that classroom management is an influential variable in teacher effectiveness (see, for example, Corbett & Wilson, 2002; Dubner, 1979; Wang et al., 1993a). Explorations of student achievement, surveys of perceptions, and meta-analyses on a range of studies have all supported the notion that effective management is a key component of effective teaching. Elements of effective classroom management include establishing routines and procedures to limit disruption and time taken away from teaching and learning, maintaining momentum and variety in instructional practices, and monitoring and responding to student activity. These elements contribute to students' active engagement in the learning process (Marzano, Marzano, & Pickering, 2003).

Research findings on the classroom management skills of effective teachers consistently outline the following elements:

• Effective teachers are more consistent and proactive in classroom management as compared to less effective teachers, who are more permissive and inconsistent (Molnar et al., 1999).

• Effective teachers establish routines for all daily tasks and needs (Bain & Jacobs, 1990).

• Effective classroom managers orchestrate smooth transitions and continuity of momentum throughout the day (Brophy & Good, 1986; Education USA Special Report, n.d.).

• Effective teachers and classroom managers strike a balance between variety and challenge in student activities (Brophy & Good, 1986).

• Effective educators have a heightened awareness of all actions and activities in the classroom (Wang et al., 1993a).

• Classroom management skills include the use of space and proximity or movement around the classroom to be near trouble spots and encourage attention (McLeod, Fisher, & Hoover, 2003; Wang et al., 1993a).

• Effective teachers limit disruption by anticipating potential problems (Emmer et al., 1980).

• Effective classroom teachers resolve minor inattention and disruptions before they become major disruptions (Covino & Iwanicki, 1996).

• Effective classroom managers are able to increase student engagement in learning and make good use of every instructional moment (Good & Brophy, 1997).

• Effective teachers seem to have eyes in the backs of their heads (Covino & Iwanicki, 1996).

Related Resources: Bain & Jacobs, 1990; Berliner, 1986; Brophy & Good, 1986; Cotton, 1999, 2000; Covino & Iwanicki, 1996; Demmon-Berger, 1986; Doyle, 1986; Education USA Special Report, n.d.; Emmer et al., 1980; Emmer et al., 2003; Fidler, 2002; Good & Brophy, 1997; Good & McCaslin, 1992; Kounin, 1970; McLeod et al., 2003; Molnar et al., 1999; Pressley, Wharton-McDonald, Allington, Block, & Morrow, 1998; Shellard & Protheroe, 2000; Sokal et al., 2003; Teddlie & Stringfield, 1993; Wang et al., 1993a, 1993b; Wong & Wong, 1998; Yamaguchi et al., 1997.

Applying Elements of Organization

Organizational skills deserve special attention in our discussion of effective classroom management and its role in effective teaching. The teacher who is organized in terms of routines, behaviors, and materials typically is better prepared for class and sets an example of organization for students that supports their learning. Emphasis on organization has been shown to contribute to effective teaching by freeing up as much as an extra hour per week from administrative or lost time that can be used for instruction.

Most effective teachers admit that rules, procedures, and routines take precedence over academic lessons during the first week of school, noting that organization takes a considerable investment of time at first but has tremendous payback benefits (Emmer et al., 2003). An exploratory study of effective versus ineffective teachers found that teachers whose students make greater achievement gains use more routines for everyday tasks than teachers whose students made less than expected achievement gains (Stronge, Tucker, & Ward, 2003). The organization of materials allows for smooth transitions between activities and increases the amount of time spent on academic tasks. Consequently, as students focus on academic engagement, the potential for behavior problems is greatly reduced.

Organized classrooms are easy to recognize. Instructors in well-organized classrooms prepare effective working environments by optimizing proximity to materials and students. Routines and procedures are established so that the classrooms seem to run automatically (McLeod, et al., 2003). Students know exactly what to do and when to do it. This orchestrated level of organization allows effective teachers to provide differentiated instruction when it is needed.

Good classroom organization is achieved in a variety of ways. For example, one elementary school uses color-coding to assist teachers and students in quickly locating materials. If multiple preparations are required of a teacher, color-coding bins or folders (one color per subject) can optimize organization. Placing commonly used materials such as scissors, staplers, tape, and crayons in easily accessible places for students saves the teacher from being the sole distributor of such resources. Dish tubs may be used to organize the materials needed for a hands-on activity and should be prepared in advance to save class time. In secondary school, science educators can designate students to serve as laboratory assistants who help prepare for lab work. In elementary school, the assignment of classroom jobs encourages responsibility, as students serve as line leaders and paper collectors on a rotating basis. Using a combination of strategies to organize the classroom can allow more class time to be allocated for instruction.

Taking the time to set up procedures for routine tasks in a classroom enables the teacher to cue students to perform them with a minimal amount of explanation. Training, feedback, and praise, however, are needed to establish the routines. Just as kindergartners must be taught what to do when the fire drill sounds, procedures must be taught so that they become automatic responses. Once taught, the routines can be adapted if the situation arises, but the groundwork is laid for a well-orchestrated classroom.

Many studies summarize these key elements of organization:

• Effective teachers handle routine tasks promptly and efficiently (Bain & Jacobs, 1990; Cotton, 2000).

Having materials prepared and ready for use in advance of the lesson, including extra materials in case of unexpected problems or sudden arrival of new students, is a mark of an organized instructor (Berendt & Koski, 1999; Brophy & Good, 1986; Emmer et al., 1980).

• Effective teachers emphasize structure in both student and lesson management (Zahorik, Halbach, Ehrle, & Molnar, 2003).

• Teachers in effective schools reported higher priority and more instructional time devoted to reading than in less effective schools (Taylor, Pearson, Clark, & Walpole, 1999).

• Creating and maintaining practical procedures allows teachers to support students in knowing what they are to do, with minimum repetition of directions (Emmer et al., 1980).

• Communicating to students the organization of space and where necessary materials are to be stored is common among effective teachers (Bain & Jacobs, 1990).

Related Resources: Bain & Jacobs, 1990; Berendt & Koski, 1999; Brophy & Good, 1986; Cotton, 1999, 2000; Covino & Iwanicki, 1996; Emmer et al., 1980; Shellard & Protheroe, 2000; Stronge et al., 2003; Taylor et al., 1999; Wang et al., 1993a, 1993b; Wong & Wong, 1998; Zahorik et al., 2003.

Managing and Responding to Student Behavior

One of the most important organizational skills an effective teacher possesses is the ability to prevent negative behavior. Studies indicate that the majority of behavior problems occur because students do not know or do not follow routines and procedures. This supports the notion that proactive classroom management is the most effective deterrent to discipline problems. Praising students, reinforcing positive behaviors, and establishing trust within the classroom builds respectful relationships between teachers and students. Disciplinary actions are rare in environments where teachers and students respect and trust each other.

One key to minimizing discipline problems is good classroom management skills. Effective teachers manage and attend to the needs of all students within the class. Unfortunately, classroom observation reports reveal that most teachers direct their attention and instruction more frequently to some students and ignore others. In the same sense, they provide more positive feedback to some while ignoring others. This type of teacher behavior increases the likelihood of student misbehavior. On the other hand, effective classroom managers are able to recognize cues from students and decide if a predetermined procedure or routine should be able to handle the behaviors. If no routine was established in advance, the teacher quickly adapts to handle the situation with little or no disruption to the other students.

Another key to preventing negative behavior is the relationship between the teacher and students. Part of building relationships with students hinges on trust. Tschannen-Moran (2000) explained the importance of trust in this way: "Without trust, students' energy is diverted toward self-protection and away from learning" (p. 4). Although a teacher may have rules established in the classroom, if students do not trust the consistency and fairness with which rules are applied, then the rules become ineffective and the teacher loses credibility, as well as the ability to manage student behavior. Therefore, characteristics of the teacher as a person from Chapter 2 relate to a teacher's effectiveness in creating a positive atmosphere in which negative behavior is minimized.

Teachers who set and reinforce clear expectations for student behavior have more success in classroom control and fewer discipline problems than those who fail to do so. Teachers realize that setting high expectations for behavior is just as important to learning as setting high expectations for academic performance (Covino & Iwanicki, 1996). High expectations for student behavior spill over into other areas of teacher effectiveness, such as responsiveness to individual student performance when planning instruction (Fuchs, Fuchs, & Phillips, 1994).

Involving students in establishing rules and procedures at the beginning of the school year is one approach effective teachers use to ensure students recognize the importance of the students' role in the classroom. Effective teachers clearly communicate and reinforce behavioral expectations. When an expectation is not met, the educator addresses the concern, gives the student an opportunity to identify the issue, and provides ample examples of other choices that the student could have made. Additionally, the teacher assists students in understanding the logic behind the rules and the reasonableness of the consequences for breaking the rules, as well as the rewards for following them. These teachers link consequences, at appropriate maturity levels, to the behavior displayed by the student (Wentzel, 2002). They handle discipline issues on an individual basis as opposed to having class consequences for the actions of a few. For situations that are unfamiliar to students, the teacher provides instructions on how to behave. Parents and administrators are involved in supporting and enforcing effective teachers' well-prepared discipline plans. Finally, effective teachers truly believe that students have the capacity to learn self-discipline.

For students in early grades, the explicitness of rules and routines is most important; for students in later grades, clarity of expectations is a more important factor (Cotton, 2000). Equally important as establishing behavioral expectations is the consistency that teachers show in carrying out responses to the breaking of rules. Such consistent responses and appropriate management help effective teachers achieve lower levels of off-task student behaviors in their classrooms. Effective teachers also use discipline to carefully manage the learning environment. Of the disciplinary situations that do arise, effective teachers are able to handle the majority of them within the classroom, without involving administrators. They realize that by reducing disciplinary problems within the classroom, they may be able to significantly increase overall student achievement. Essentially, the less disciplining that takes place, the more time there is for instruction; the more time there is for instruction, the more students learn.

Research on effective teachers' ability to efficiently manage student discipline consistently indicates the following:

• The effective teacher minimizes discipline time and accentuates instructional time (Bain & Jacobs, 1990; Brophy & Good, 1986; Covino & Iwanicki, 1996).

• The time a teacher spends on disciplining students inversely affects student achievement outcomes (Education USA Special Report, n.d.).

• A strong teacher-student relationship is the key to reducing discipline problems and correcting behaviors and decision making, both in and out of the classroom (Marzano, 2003; Wolk, 2002).

• The effective teacher interprets and responds to inappropriate behaviors promptly (Emmer et al., 1980; Good & Brophy, 1997; Zahorik et al., 2003).

• The effective teacher holds individual students accountable for their behavior (Kohn, 1996).

• The effective teacher maintains clear rules and procedures and establishes credibility with students through fair and consistent implementation of discipline (Peart & Campbell, 1999; Shellard & Protheroe, 2000; Wharton-McDonald, Pressley, & Hampston, 1998).

  • The effective teacher reinforces and reiterates the expectations for positive behavior (Good & Brophy, 1997) and uses strategies to redirect negative student behavior (McLeod et al., 2003; Walker-Dalhouse, 2005).

Related Resources: Bain & Jacobs, 1990; Bloom, 1984; Brophy & Good, 1986; Cotton, 1999, 2000; Covino & Iwanicki, 1996; Doyle, 1986; Education USA Special Report, n.d.; Emmer et al., 1980; Fuchs et al., 1994; Good & Brophy, 1997; Hanushek, 1971; Hoffman & Levak, 2003; Marzano, 2003; McLeod et al., 2003; Peart & Campbell, 1999; Shellard & Protheroe, 2000; Tschannen-Moran, 2000; Walker-Dalhouse, 2005; Wang et al., 1993a, 1993b; Wharton-McDonald et al., 1998; Wolk, 2002; Wong & Wong, 1998; Yamaguchi et al., 1997; Zahorik et al., 2003.

Teachers of At-Risk Students: Classroom Management and Organization

In addition to demonstrating their adeptness at classroom management and organization, effective teachers of at-risk students often emphasize creating and maintaining a *positive* learning environment. The teacher begins to establish this positive environment on the first day of school. The first step is to begin building positive relationships with individual students, as described in the previous chapter. Howard (2002) supports the notion that not only should the environment be positive, but it should also be family-like. This relationship establishes clear boundaries between the roles of teacher and student. Quite clearly, maintaining positive relationships with all students, and especially at-risk students, is necessary for a positive learning environment.

The students themselves see the need for orderly classrooms. In a survey of urban students, researchers found that students perceive good teachers as those who maintain control in the classroom (Corbett & Wilson, 2002). An orderly classroom means the articulation of positive expectations and the rewards and consequences associated with those expectations.

Consequently, effective teachers create warm and cooperative classroom climates by developing rules and having high student involvement. Teachers and students have clearly established roles along with a caring atmosphere (Taylor, Pressley, & Pearson, 2000). When a discipline issue arises, these teachers deal with the issue in a calm and quiet manner, reminding students of appropriate behavior in inconspicuous ways (Knapp, Shields, & Turnbull,

1992). This could include a quiet whisper, a nod of the head, or a hand on the desk. They also reinforce positive behavior using tangible rewards. While these qualities are important in working with all students, it appears that they need to be underlined in working with at-risk students. The following research summaries underscore the importance of these qualities:

• At-risk students value teachers who control the classroom and reward positive behavior (Corbett & Wilson, 2002; Pressley et al., 2004).

• A significant factor associated with reading achievement for African American students includes maintaining an orderly classroom (Armor et al., 1976).

• Students in effective classrooms are aware of classroom rules and the expectations of behavior (Hamre & Pianta, 2005).

• Students who reported satisfaction with their school received fewer verbal reprimands than students who reported dissatisfaction with their school (Baker, 1999).

• Effective teachers of at-risk students have high expectations for student behavior and display and enforce classroom rules (Bridglall & Gordon, 2003; Fuchs et al., 1994; Pressley et al., 2004; Taylor et al., 2000).

• Effective teachers create positive, warm classroom climates (Taylor et al., 2000, Walker-Dalhouse, 2005; Waxman, Shwu-Yong, Anderson, & Weinstein, 1997).

Related Resources: Armor et al., 1976; Baker, 1999; Bridglall & Gordon, 2003; Corbett & Wilson, 2002; Fuchs et al., 1994; Hamre & Pianta, 2005; Howard, 2002; Knapp et al., 1992; Pressley et al., 2004; Taylor et al., 2000; Walker-Dalhouse, 2005; Waxman et al., 1997.

Teachers of High-Ability Students: Classroom Management and Organization

Gifted students recognize and appreciate a teacher's organization of the classroom and of learning experiences. Because differentiation for gifted learners is so important, the teacher must be able to organize the classroom so that the environment is conducive to constant activity that is likely to be quite divergent in nature.

Effective teachers of the gifted recognize that behavioral issues must be handled in a way that takes into account the social and emotional needs of high-ability learners. Gifted students, like any other students, can be inattentive, competitive, silly, or disruptive, and may lack the social skills to deal with other students or adults in an appropriate manner (Hunt & Seney, 2001). Teachers must assist students by teaching them techniques to deal with their own behaviors, as well as by examining the possible contributing factors to students' behavior, including the appropriateness of the instructional experience for the needs of the student.

Teachers of gifted and talented students must be able to multitask—for example, attending to one group's request to consult with a NASA expert online while remembering to check on an individual student's progress in conducting an experiment. Students may be working in groups or they may be working independently. The students may be collaborating formally or they may be consulting one another for advice. Resources in different areas of the room must be available and organized in a manner that supports a positive learning environment. In other words, effective teachers of gifted students must be especially comfortable with the role of facilitator of learning rather than giver of knowledge. Additionally, if rules and procedures underlying this flurry of activity are not established, chaos can break out in the classroom.

Effective teachers of the gifted do the following:

• Maintain order through classroom organization (Dubner, 1979; Eyre et al., 2002).

• Define expectations for behavior (Nikakis, 2002) by involving students in setting rules and procedures for class norms during discussions and activities (Maddux et al., 1985).

• Provide a rich variety of resources in the classroom (Johnsen, Haensley, Ryser, & Ford, 2002; Johnsen & Ryser, 1996; VanTassel-Baska & Little, 2003).

• Organize the classroom to encourage interaction among students (Callahan, 2001; Lee-Corbin & Denicolo, 1998).

• Are able to manage students as they conduct research, original investigations, and independent studies (Feldhusen, 1991).

• Recognize that inappropriate behaviors may reflect inappropriate instructional placement and use appropriate intervention techniques when behavioral issues arise (Hunt & Seney, 2001).

• Are more skilled than untrained teachers of the gifted in creating a positive classroom environment (Hansen & Feldhusen, 1994).

Related Resources: Callahan, 2001; Dubner, 1979; Eyre et al., 2002; Feldhusen, 1991; Grant, 2002; Hansen & Feldhusen, 1994; Hunt & Seney, 2001; Johnsen & Ryser, 1996; Johnsen et al., 2002; Lee-Corbin & Denicolo, 1998; Maddux et al., 1985; Nikakis, 2002; VanTassel-Baska & Little, 2003.

Figure 3.1
Key References for Classroom Management and Organization

Reference	Classroom Management	Key Elements of Organization	Disciplining Students	Teachers of At-Risk Students	Teachers of High-Ability Students
Bain & Jacobs, 1990	•	•	•		
Baker, 1999			•	•	
Berendt & Koski, 1999		•			
Berliner, 1986	•				
Bloom, 1984			•		
Brophy & Good, 1986	•	•	•		
Callahan, 2001		•			•
Corbett & Wilson, 2002	•		•	•	
Cotton, 1999	•	•	•		
Cotton, 2000	•	•	•		
Covino & Iwanicki, 1996	•	•	•		
Demmon-Berger, 1986	•				
Doyle, 1986	•		•		
Dubner, 1979		•			•
ERS, 2000	•	•	•		
Education USA Special Report, n.d.	•		•		
Emmer et al., 1980	•	•	•		
Feldhusen, 1991		•			•
Fuchs et al., 1994			•	•	
Good & Brophy, 1997	•		•		
Good & McCaslin, 1992	•				
Hamre & Pianta, 2005	•		•	•	
Hansen & Feldhusen, 1994	•				•
Hanushek, 1971			•		
Howard, 2002	•			•	
Johnsen et al., 2002		•			•

Reference	Classroom Management	Key Elements of Organization	Disciplining Students	Teachers of At-Risk Students	Teachers of High-Ability Students
Johnson, 1997	●				
Knapp et al., 1992			●	●	
Kounin, 1970	●				
Maddux et al., 1985	●				●
Marzano, 2003			●		
Marzano et al., 2003	●				
McLeod et al., 2003	●	●			
Nikakis, 2002	●				●
Peart & Campbell, 1999	●			●	
Pressley et al., 2004	●		●	●	
Sokal et al., 2003	●				
Taylor et al., 2000	●		●	●	
Teddlie & Stringfield, 1993	●				
Walker-Dalhouse, 2005	●			●	
Wang et al., 1993a	●	●	●		
Wang et al., 1993b	●	●	●		
Waxman et al., 1997	●			●	
Wentzel, 2002			●		
Wharton-McDonald et al., 1998			●		
Wong & Wong, 1998	●	●	●		
Yamaguchi et al., 1997	●		●		
Zahorik et al., 2003	●	●	●		

Figure 3.1 *Continued*
Key References for Classroom Management and Organization

4

Planning and Organizing
for Instruction

Morgan transformed the physical look of the school, from her classroom out to the halls, from the walls to the ceiling, and even into the bus parking lot. She was an amazing artist in her own right, but she was also an extraordinarily effective teacher. Not only did her art lessons involve planning what techniques and media students would focus on, but she also met with core content teachers (math, science, social studies, and English) to link her instruction with theirs. Morgan planned for her classes to work outside of the classroom by painting murals around the school themed to the content areas. For her students to create these instructional masterpieces, she carefully monitored her meager art supplies and found ways to make them stretch, such as buying the "oops" paint (i.e., paint that is returned to the store) at the hardware store for big projects. Her students developed skills, shared their talents, and left a legacy to the school.

Teaching is a complex activity that involves careful preparation and planning objectives and activities on an hourly, daily, and weekly basis. In addition, long-term planning ensures coverage of curriculum across a marking period, semester, and year. Further, effective educators demonstrate high expectations for students and select strategies to propel the students' learning. Beyond planning and preparation of materials, effective organizing for instruction also involves the development of a conscious orientation toward teaching and learning as the central focus of classroom activity. Teaching and learning as a focus must be consistently communicated to students in the classroom and to observers. This chapter explores elements of organizing and orienting for instruction that have been identified as part of effective teaching practice. Figure 4.1, at the end of this chapter, outlines key references relating to these elements.

Focusing on Instruction

The effective teacher recognizes academic instruction as central to his or her role. This focus on instruction guides not only the teacher's own planning and classroom behavior, but also comes across clearly to students and represents *the* major element in a robust learning environment. A teacher may say to students, "It is my job to see that you succeed," or, "I want you to be prepared for life beyond the schoolhouse door." Although effective teachers believe that students must be challenged, they also realize that students need to experience success.

Several studies have emphasized the importance of a focus on high-quality instruction in supporting student achievement, including the following findings and conclusions:

• Effective teachers see consistency and organization in their classrooms as important because they allow the central focus of classroom time to be on teaching and learning (Bain & Jacobs, 1990).

• Effective teachers give high priority to foundational academic goals related to benchmarks or standards (Cawelti, 2004) and give secondary attention to higher-order personal and social goals (Zahorik et al., 2003).

• Effective teachers who consistently prioritize instruction and student learning as the central purposes of schooling communicate an enthusiasm and dedication to learning that students reflect in their own behavior and practice (Bain & Jacobs, 1990).

• Effective teachers reinforce their focus on instruction through their allocation of time to the teaching and learning process, and through their expectations for student learning (Brophy & Good, 1986; Cawelti, 2004; Cotton, 2000; Covino & Iwanicki, 1996; Molnar et al., 1999).

• The amount of time students spend engaged in learning experiences, together with the quality of the instruction, is positively associated with student learning (Walberg, 1984).

Related Resources: Bain & Jacobs, 1990; Berliner & Rosenshine, 1977; Brophy & Good, 1986; Cawelti, 1999, 2004; Cotton, 1999, 2000; Covino & Iwanicki, 1996; Molnar et al., 1999; Walberg, 1984; Wang et al., 1993a, 1993b; Zahorik et al., 2003.

Maximizing Instructional Time

Time is one of the most challenging constraints a teacher faces in trying to achieve curricular goals and meet the needs of all students, while managing the administrative tasks that are a necessary responsibility of the job. According to various studies, teachers spend about 70 percent of their classroom instruction time on the core curriculum. The remaining 30 percent is spent on completing such tasks as collecting money for the school fund-raiser, enforcing classroom rules and procedures, participating in fire drills and schoolwide assemblies, and listening to schoolwide announcements (Meek, 2003; NCES, 1997). A study of U.S. mathematics lessons revealed that lessons were interrupted by a public announcement 29 percent of the time (Hiebert et al., 2005). Nonetheless, effective teachers do manage to maximize instruction by their thoughtful and careful use of time.

Research has demonstrated that student achievement is higher in classes where instructional time is maximized (see, for example, Taylor et al., 1999; Walberg, 1984). The effective teacher prioritizes instruction, a process that is accomplished partially through allocation of time. One illustration of how effective teachers best use the scarce commodity of time is in smoothly orchestrated classroom transitions; they remain involved with the students during the entire class period from start to finish, allowing for no idle or down time.

Use of time can be optimized in the classroom by careful planning or by using pacing materials. Students often want to know what is coming up next week or next month. Therefore, having a scope and sequence helps the teacher to plan and addresses student needs for information. For example, the use of calendars for long-term, weekly, and daily planning, in addition to providing a visual reminder to the teacher, can help students plan for work. Effective teachers are not only organized, but also they convey this vital skill to their students. Sharing with students how the teacher organizes time can serve as a model for students to assist in their own planning, thus equipping them with tools of success in the larger world and instilling in them habits of efficiency.

Staging areas help teachers maximize time by organizing materials for upcoming activities or common but unpredictable occurrences. For example, a list on the back of the door of what the teacher needs to do if a new student arrives fulfills a dual purpose: the new student feels that the teacher is organized, and the teacher feels prepared for the student. Another time-saving device is to use a designated place to keep materials such as attendance cards, hall passes, and extra paper. This saves time because the teacher does not have to search for the items. In essence, in the effective classroom there is a place for everything and everything is in its place.

Establishing a pattern so that students can anticipate academic transitions reduces the loss of instructional time. Students observe the routine and know what will occur. For example, a teacher who uses a class warm-up activity that is displayed on the board or at work stations when students enter the room accomplishes the following multiple purposes:

• Gives students a way to constructively use their time during a class change or morning arrival.

• Prepares the students for the day's activities.

• Offers the teacher an opportunity to take roll or respond to a note from a parent at the start of class while the students are engaged.

• Makes use of time that otherwise would have been lost.

• Provides a focus for the first few minutes of class that can be extended into an introduction for the lesson.

Some teachers follow the same routine virtually every class period, as they review homework, introduce a new concept, use the new skill in an activity, and, if there is time, have independent practice. Other teachers use visual cues to signal a transition as opposed to a routine set of activities. For example, playing music, ringing a bell, or flickering the lights may signal to students that they need to complete a task before the class can move to the next activity. Techniques and routines such as these can capture minutes a day that add up to instructional hours over the course of the school year.

Studies reveal that effective teachers exercise varying techniques and strategies to ensure maximum learning time. The practices suggested above and those that follow support the effective teacher's overall emphasis on instruction. Additionally, they provide the framework for maximizing not only instructional time, but also students' time on task. Effective teachers do the following:

• Follow a consistent schedule and maintain the procedures and routines established at the beginning of the year (Berendt & Koski, 1999; Brophy & Good, 1986).

• Handle administrative tasks quickly and efficiently (Zahorik et al., 2003).

• Prepare materials in advance (Bain & Jacobs, 1990; Walls, Nardi, von Minden, & Hoffman, 2002).

• Make clear and smooth transitions (Brophy & Good, 1986; Wang et al., 1993b; Zahorik et al., 2003).

• Maintain momentum within and across lessons (Brophy & Good, 1986; Cotton, 2000).

• Limit disruptions and interruptions through appropriate behavioral management techniques (Cotton, 2000; Education USA Special Report, n.d.; Wang et al., 1993b).

Related Resources: Bain & Jacobs, 1990; Berendt & Koski, 1999; Brophy & Good, 1986; Cawelti, 1999; Cotton, 1999, 2000; Covino & Iwanicki, 1996; Education USA Special Report, n.d.; Good & Brophy, 1997; Hiebert et al., 2005; Meek, 2003; NCES, 1997; Walker, 1998; Walls et al., 2002; Wang et al., 1993a, 1993b; Zahorik et al., 2003.

Expecting Students to Achieve

The previous chapter discussed the importance of the effective teacher's practice of clear, specific expectations for student behavior. However, clarifying behavioral expectations isn't enough; an accompanying clear and consistent focus on achievement expectations is also essential to academic success. Effective teachers believe in their students and expect all of them to learn, regardless of their skill levels and starting points. Moreover, effective teachers believe that students can learn; therefore, their students do learn. Unfortunately, this self-fulfilling prophecy works both ways. For example, if a teacher believes that students are low-performing, unreachable, and unable to learn, the students perform poorly, seem unreachable, and do not learn.

The expectations a teacher holds for students, whether consciously or subconsciously, are demonstrated through the teacher's interactions with the students during instruction. Research on teacher expectations has demonstrated that for the students in the bottom third of the class, many teachers have significantly lower achievement expectations and provide much less encouragement. Conversely, students in the top third of the class get the most teacher attention and encouragement (Good & Brophy, 1997). Student academic performance is influenced by a teacher's expectations and goals for student achievement (Wentzel, 2002). This pattern of teacher behavior can be eliminated through self-observation (videotaped or audiotaped lessons) and self-awareness, so teachers can then bestow the benefits of attention and encouragement on all students.

In several studies, teacher expectations have been shown to relate to student achievement, including the following findings and conclusions:

• High expectations are identified as a key component of student success (Cotton, 2000; Education USA Special Report, n.d.; Johnson, 1997; Peart & Campbell, 1999; Porter & Brophy, 1988).

• High expectations represent an overall orientation toward improvement and growth in the classroom (Good & Brophy, 1997; Mason et al., 1992), which has been demonstrated to be a defining characteristic of benchmark schools (Cotton, 2000).

• Some studies have suggested that subtle communication of lower expectations for certain students from teachers can limit achievement, while clearly articulated high expectations can become a self-fulfilling prophecy (Good & Brophy, 1997).

• Effective teachers not only express and clarify expectations for student achievement, but also stress student responsibility and accountability for striving to meet those expectations (Peart & Campbell, 1999).

Related Resources: Bloom, 1984; Cawelti, 1999, 2004; Cotton, 1999, 2000; Covino & Iwanicki, 1996; Education USA Special Report, n.d.; Good & Brophy, 1997; Good & McCaslin, 1992; Johnson, 1997; Mason et al., 1992; Peart & Campbell, 1999; Porter & Brophy, 1988; Price, 2000; Tschannen-Moran, Hoy, & Hoy, 1998; Wang et al., 1993a, 1993b; Wong & Wong, 1998.

Planning and Preparing for Instruction

Teachers determine how content and skills are delivered in the classroom. School district curriculum, state standards, and national standards play a role in what students should learn (Jackson & Davis, 2000), but it falls to the teacher to structure how students should learn it. Planning is a deliberate process that results in teachers being well-prepared prior to walking through the classroom door for the day (Wharton-McDonald et al., 1998). Organizing time and preparing materials in advance of instruction have been noted as important aspects of effective teaching. Individual and team planning are beneficial to creating valuable learning experiences for students. Team planning allows teachers to collaboratively examine important issues and to develop a collective approach to instruction (Jackson & Davis, 2000). Both the organization of time and the preparation of materials are components of the broader practice of planning carefully for instruction. Once the plans are developed, evidence suggests that effective teachers follow the instructional or lesson plan while continuously adjusting it to fit the needs of different students.

During their instructional planning time, effective teachers assess or recall students' preconceptions and misconceptions about the subject matter. Pre-assessments can help gauge students' prior knowledge of the material. Effective teachers take into account the abilities of their students and the students' strengths and weaknesses as well as their interest levels. A study of teacher expectations revealed that teachers who had high classroom standards also planned in response to individual student performance, which was then linked to student achievement (Fuchs et al., 1994). Teachers who plan instruction based on student performance and interest levels meet both the affective needs of students and their cognitive needs.

Novice teachers have more difficulty responding to individual student needs in their planning. They tend to develop a "one-size-fits-all" approach to planning, whereas more experienced teachers build in differentiation and contingencies at different points during the lesson (Good & Brophy, 1997; Jay, 2002; Livingston & Borko, 1989; Sabers, Cushing, & Berliner, 1991). To further assist with meeting individual needs, effective teachers typically plan a blend of whole-group, small-group, and individualized instruction. Planning for instruction involves careful preparation for specific lessons, as well as long-term planning to ensure coverage of curriculum. Some studies have demonstrated that student achievement is related to the amount of content coverage a teacher accomplishes (see, for example, Dunkin, 1978; Dunkin & Doenau, 1980). Careful, deliberate planning maximizes the amount of content a teacher is able to cover.

Effective teachers also evaluate resources to use when teaching a unit or lesson. They use criteria such as appropriateness for grade level; alignment to national, state, or local standards; accuracy of information contained within the resource; the time allowed for the lesson or unit; and the learning benefits that come from using the resource (Buttram & Waters, 1997). For example, when showing a video on the causes of the Civil War, the teacher may select only a poignant quote or section from the video, rather than showing the entire segment. Teachers also recognize that other adults can be a resource for the learning process. They coordinate the participation of adults in order to promote student engagement (Pressley et al., 1998; Wharton-McDonald et al., 1998). In summary, effective teachers maximize the instructional benefits of resources while minimizing time allocated to less relevant or unnecessary material.

Since students learn at different rates, effective teachers plan academic enrichment and remediation opportunities for students. Through the teacher's knowledge of the students, it is possible to offer alternatives to a student or a small group of students who have mastered the material faster than the rest of the class. These students can study the concept on a deeper level or apply the concept in a different way. Students who may lack the prerequisite knowledge or skills need the teacher to give them time to learn the foundational material on which to build the new piece. Providing meaningful experiences for all students to learn is a goal of planning.

By planning a unit that takes into account the students' prior knowledge and prior performance as well as their learning styles, a teacher can implement effective vehicles for instruction. Teachers tend to teach in the manner that they themselves learn best; however, effective teachers stretch beyond that comfort zone to incorporate different learning styles. For example, during a lesson on the water cycle, the teacher may solicit ideas of what the students already know, run an action simulation in which students roll dice to determine where in the water cycle the students will go next, incorporate a writing experience where the students personify the water droplet to tell about their journey, graph where the droplets went, and then discuss what they observed and compare it to what they had previously thought. Whatever the unit, students benefit if the material can be connected to something they are already familiar with from prior school experiences or real-life situations. In the water cycle activity, the teacher can take what the students already knew, build upon it, and address some of their misconceptions. Conscientious planning for student instruction and engagement is a key to connecting the classroom to future success for students.

Research indicates that instructional planning for effective teaching includes the following elements:

• Identifying clear lesson and learning objectives while carefully linking activities to them, which is essential for effectiveness (Cotton, 2000; Wang et al., 1993b; Wharton-McDonald et al., 1998).

• Creating quality assignments, which is positively associated with quality instruction and quality student work (Clare, 2000).

• Planning lessons that have clear goals, are logically structured, and progress through the content step-by-step (Rosenshine, 1986; Zahorik et al., 2003).

• Planning the instructional strategies to be deployed in the classroom and the timing of these strategies (Cotton, 2000; Johnson, 1997).

• Using advance organizers, graphic organizers, and outlines to plan for effective instructional delivery (Marzano, Norford, Paynter, Pickering, & Gaddy, 2001; Wang et al., 1993b).

• Considering student attention spans and learning styles when designing lessons (Bain & Jacobs, 1990).

• Systematically developing objectives, questions, and activities that reflect higher-level and lower-level cognitive skills as appropriate for the content and the students (Brophy & Good, 1986; Porter & Brophy, 1988).

Related Resources: Bain & Jacobs, 1990; Berliner & Rosenshine, 1977; Brookhart & Loadman, 1992; Brophy & Good, 1986; Clare, 2000; Cotton, 1999, 2000; Covino & Iwanicki, 1996; Darling-Hammond, 2000, 2001; Education USA Special Report, n.d.; Emmer et al., 1980; Good & Brophy, 1997; Good & McCaslin, 1992; Jackson & Davis, 2000; Johnson, 1997; Livingston & Borko, 1989; Marzano, Norford, et al., 2001; Marzano, Pickering, & McTighe, 1993; Porter & Brophy, 1988; Pressley et al., 1998; Rosenshine,1986; Sabers et al., 1991; Wharton-McDonald et al., 1998; Zahorik et al., 2003.

Teachers of At-Risk Students: Planning and Organizing for Instruction

Planning and organizing instruction for at-risk students mirrors those characteristics that have already been discussed; however, the literature does reveal aspects of planning that seem to be especially important for at-risk students. These aspects include the following:

• Planning for and protecting instructional time
• Maintaining high expectations
• Examining resources and lessons for bias
• Using a variety of instructional activities to enhance student learning

Planning for instruction involves planning meaningful lessons that communicate high expectations to students (Bernard, 2003). A strong indicator for students at risk of not succeeding or dropping out of school is the expectations of the adults that surround them (Wahlage & Rutter, 1986). Additionally, effective teachers do not focus merely on basic skills, even if students are lacking in these skills. Instead, they plan for mastery of the basics while incorporating higher-level, metacognitive thinking into the lesson. This is counter to the belief that "for most children in poverty, academically challenging work in mathematics and literacy should be postponed until they are 'ready'—that is, until they have acquired full mastery of basic skills" (Knapp et al., 1992, p. i). By focusing on only lower-level basic skills, teachers communicate lower expectations. Consequently, effective teachers of at-risk students plan and organize instruction in such a way that students are exposed to the content and skills necessary to achieve.

Effective teachers of at-risk students do the following:

• Expect students to do their work and do not accept excuses (Bernard, 2003, Corbett & Wilson, 2002; Freel, 1998).

• Are on task every minute they are in the classroom and make sure students have time to learn (Bennett et al., 2004; Pressley et al., 2004; Wenglinsky, 2004).

• Examine the nature of the lesson and cultural assumptions that negatively affect at-risk students (Pransky & Bailey, 2002).

• Use pacing guides and timelines in order to align curriculum (Lewis, 2001).

• Plan for a variety of activities, including individualized instruction, student-led activities, student-centered learning time, and infusion of technology, if available (Day, 2002; Taylor, Pearson, Peterson, & Rodriquez, 2003).

Related Resources: Bennett et al., 2004; Bernard, 2003; Corbett & Wilson, 2002; Day, 2002; Knapp et al., 1992; Lewis, 2001; Pransky & Bailey, 2002; Pressley et al., 2004; Taylor et al., 2003; Wahlage & Rutter, 1986; Wenglinsky, 2004.

Teachers of High-Ability Students: Planning and Organizing for Instruction

Planning for high-ability learners involves taking into account the unique needs and abilities of the students, content that must be mastered, and effective strategies to use with them. Effective teachers of high-ability students use methods such as acceleration, content modification, or curriculum compacting in order to provide enriching, differentiated activities that foster students' academic growth. For example, a teacher can give a pre-assessment to determine the content and skills that students have already mastered so that valuable academic learning time is not squandered and students are not bored with learning information they already know or practicing skills they have already accomplished.

Content for gifted learners is often organized so that students can discover, experiment, and figure things out on their own. Additionally, learning experiences characterized by abstraction and complexity are needed to provide mental challenge for the learners (Hutchinson, 2004).

Unfortunately, gifted learners too frequently are given busywork to fill time (Johnson, 2000; Maker & Neilson, 1996). Effective teachers of the gifted understand that this type of busywork is counterproductive to establishing a positive learning environment. By planning differentiated activities and organizing content in such a way that encourages exploration, the effective teacher does not need to be concerned about what to do with students when they finish their work early. This approach to gifted instruction fosters growth in gifted students, rather than inhibiting it.

Effective teachers of gifted students do the following:

• Match task complexities and individual skills in the planning process, leading to greater student motivation and engagement (Csikszentmihalyi et al., 1993).

• Exhibit competency in the selection and use of materials (Hansen & Feldhusen, 1994; Nelson & Prindle, 1992; Story, 1985), particularly the ability to select appropriate high-level materials (Shore & Delcourt, 1996), and choose appropriate resources to use with students who are both gifted and diverse (Ford & Trotman, 2001).

• Facilitate access to needed resources, including providing access to advanced classes and materials, collaborating with other teachers and content-area experts, and connecting students with content-area experts and mentors (Shore & Delcourt, 1996; Westberg & Archambault, 1997).

• Use time well in the classroom (Heath, 1997; Silverman, 1995).

• Have high expectations of performance and expect their students to reach or exceed those high expectations (Bloom, 1985).

Related Resources: Bloom, 1985; Csikszentmihalyi et al., 1993; Hansen & Feldhusen, 1994; Heath, 1997; Hutchinson, 2004; Johnson, 2000; Maker & Nielson, 1996; Nelson & Prindle, 1992; Shore & Delcourt, 1996; Silverman, 1995; Story, 1985; Westberg & Archambault, 1997.

Figure 4.1						
Key References for Planning and Organizing for Instruction						
Reference	**Importance of Instruction**	**Time Allocation**	**Teacher Expectation**	**Planning for Instruction**	**Teachers of At-Risk Students**	**Teachers of High-Ability Students**
Bain & Jacobs, 1990	•	•		•		
Bennett et al., 2004	•	•			•	
Berendt & Koski, 1999	•	•				
Berliner & Rosenshine, 1977	•			•		
Bernard, 2003			•		•	
Bloom, 1984			•			
Bloom, 1985			•			•
Brookhart & Loadman, 1992				•		
Brophy & Good, 1986	•	•				
Cawelti, 1999	•	•	•			
Cawelti, 2004	•	•	•			
Corbett & Wilson, 2002			•		•	
Cotton, 1999	•	•	•			
Cotton, 2000	•	•	•			
Covino & Iwanicki, 1996	•	•	•			
Csikszentmihalyi et al., 1993				•		•
Darling-Hammond, 2000				•		
Darling-Hammond, 2001				•		
Day, 2002				•	•	
Education USA Special Report, n.d.		•	•	•		
Emmer et al., 1980				•		
Ford & Trotman, 2001				•		•
Freel, 1998			•			•
Good & Brophy, 1997		•	•			
Good & McCaslin, 1992			•	•		

Figure 4.1 *Continued*
Key References for Planning and Organizing for Instruction

Reference	Importance of Instruction	Time Allocation	Teacher Expectation	Planning for Instruction	Teachers of At-Risk Students	Teachers of High-Ability Students
Hansen & Feldhusen, 1994				•		•
Heath, 1997		•				•
Holt-Reynolds, 1999	•					
Hutchinson, 2004				•		•
Jay, 2002				•		
Johnson, 1997			•	•		
Knapp et al., 1992			•	•	•	
Lewis, 2001				•	•	
Livingston & Borko, 1989				•		
Marzano et al., 1993				•		
Marzano, Norford, et al., 2001				•		
Mason et al., 1992			•			
Meek, 2003		•				
Molnar et al., 1999	•					
NCES, 1997		•				
Nelson & Prindle, 1992				•		•
Peart & Campbell, 1999			•			
Porter & Brophy, 1988			•	•		
Pransky & Bailey, 2002				•	•	
Pressley et al., 1998	•			•	•	
Price, 2000			•			
Rosenshine, 1986				•		
Sabers et al., 1991				•		
Shore & Delcourt, 1996				•		•
Silverman, 1995		•				•
Taylor et al., 2003				•	•	

Figure 4.1 *Continued* **Key References for Planning and Organizing for Instruction**	Importance of Instruction	Time Allocation	Teacher Expectation	Planning for Instruction	Teachers of At-Risk Students	Teachers of High-Ability Students
Reference						
Tschannen-Moran et al., 1998			•			
Wahlage & Rutter, 1986			•		•	
Walker, 1998		•				
Walls et al., 2002		•				
Wang et al., 1993a	•	•	•			
Wang et al., 1993b	•	•	•			
Wenglinsky, 2004		•		•	•	
Westberg & Archambault, 1997				•		•
Wharton-McDonald et al., 1998				•		
Wong & Wong, 1998			•			
Zahorik et al., 2003	•	•		•		

5

Implementing Instruction

Kaz's physical education students change into gym clothes, exit the locker room, and start jogging warm-up laps around the gym, which stop after the last student out of the locker room completes one lap. A whistle blows once and students immediately assume their line positions for a series of stretches that are part of a well-established routine. Different students take turns leading the stretches while Kaz checks sick notes, tardy slips, and attendance. He then tells the class that they will be focusing on basketball skill development for the day. He points to different parts of the gym and explains that there is a skill card at each station and that students will rotate through each station twice. Each station focuses on a different skill: passing, dribbling, shooting, shuttle run, rules, and critique. Each line goes to a different station and begins. A couple of minutes later, Kaz blows the whistle twice and the students stop. He tells the students to designate a student coach at each station; that person is to record students' accuracy and progress with the various skills. At the rules station, students use flash cards to quiz each other about basketball rules. At the critique station, Kaz shows students videotaped segments from a college basketball game and models how to critique the player's performance. Then he gives the students guided practice and tells them to offer constructive criticism to each other during the skill drills. Periodically, the whistle blows and students change stations. At the end of the class, Kaz collects the cards and solicits student comments about strengths and areas in which they still need further development.

Beyond teacher training, beyond rapport with students, and beyond skills in classroom management and organization, what do effective teachers actually do in the classroom? All of the previous chapters focus on the important personal qualities and social and organizational behaviors that surround the teaching process. Undoubtedly, a teacher's preparation, relationships with students, and classroom management techniques are inextricably linked with classroom success. When it comes to assessing a teacher's effectiveness, however, there is nothing more important to consider than the actual act of teaching.

While this chapter is intended to highlight an effective teacher's need to possess and use a repertoire of effective instructional strategies, to communicate effectively, and to support student engagement in the teaching and learning process, it is not an encyclopedia of what works and what doesn't in the classroom. Indeed, the contextual issues related to the art of teaching defy the creation of a single list of effective instructional behaviors. Rather, what is intended here is to provide a fundamental underpinning for academic success. In relation to this purpose, the chapter provides an overview of the effective teacher's instructional practice, focusing on research-based elements of teaching. Figure 5.1, at the end of the chapter, outlines key references relating to these elements.

Use of Instructional Strategies

After instruction has been planned and the classroom prepared, teachers must begin to actually interact academically with students and with the curriculum: they must teach. Many elements of the teaching process have been linked to effectiveness in teaching, including the strategies teachers use, the clarity of their explanation of material, and the types of questions they ask. In addition, the methods teachers use to keep students focused and engaged are clearly important in implementing instruction effectively.

A teacher's repertoire of teaching strategies is a significant element of overall effectiveness. Studies emphasize the importance of successfully implementing strategies appropriate to the content and instructional goals as well as the initial planning that precedes instructional delivery (see, for example, Molnar et al., 1999; Taylor et al., 1999). The literature on instruction suggests that students whose teachers develop and regularly integrate inquiry-based problems, hands-on learning activities, critical thinking skills, and assessments into daily lessons consistently outperform their peers.

Flexibility and adeptness with a variety of teaching strategies contribute to teacher effectiveness. Effective teachers are constantly searching for group instructional strategies that are as effective as one-on-one tutoring. Direct teaching is one example of an effective instructional technique; studies illustrate the effectiveness of other teaching strategies as well (Berliner & Rosenshine, 1977; Randall, Sekulski, & Silberg, 2003; Zahorik et al., 2003). As one educational researcher explained, the ability to vary strategies increases a teacher's effectiveness: "We do our kids a disservice by choosing one pedagogy and using it all the time" (Hoff, 2003, p. 8). Additionally, effective teachers use appropriate teaching strategies based on the content, the students, and other factors such as time and resources. For example, a study of the effectiveness of instructional strategies found that more effective teachers use direct instruction, but most effective teachers use both direct instruction and experiential learning techniques (Zahorik et al., 2003).

Teachers who successfully employ a range of strategies reach more students because they tap into more learning styles and student interests (Tomlinson, 2000). They also can use different strategies to ensure that concepts are well understood. Effective teachers routinely combine instructional techniques that involve individual, small-group, and whole-class instruction. This allows them to monitor and pace instruction based on the individual needs of students.

Some of the strategies and activities deemed effective in terms of promoting student achievement include direct teaching as well as guided and independent practice. Studies indicate that using manipulatives along with an integrative approach to problem solving in mathematics improves student performance on standardized assessments. The use of concept mapping and graphic organizers to promote students' understanding and retention of content are also factors related to effective teaching. Furthermore, effective teachers consistently note problem solving across the curriculum as an important aspect of their success.

Modeling and coaching are additional characteristics of an effective teacher's repertoire (Allington, 2002; Taylor et al., 1999). Teachers model behaviors they expect in their students. For example, a history teacher models historical inquiry by examining contrasting accounts of a historical event. A reading teacher models positive reading behaviors by reviewing main ideas or relating the pictures in the book to the words on the page when reading to a large group of children. Consequently, when students practice these behaviors, effective teachers are able to coach students along the way.

In addition to applying basic principles in their lessons, effective teachers stress the importance of higher mental processes, such as problem-solving techniques, analytical thinking skills, and creativity. They use longer and more complex assignments in order to challenge students and engage them in learning (Allington, 2002). These skills enable students to relate their learning to real-life situations and incorporate concepts into their long-term memory. Other important instructional variables found to affect student achievement include using student ideas and eliciting student comments.

The following findings related to instructional strategies are supported by the existing research:

• Lecturing, a common teaching strategy, is an effort to quickly cover the material; however, it often overloads and overwhelms students with data, making it likely that they will confuse the facts presented (Palmer, 1990).

• Teachers who use hands-on learning strategies have students who outperform their peers on the National Assessment of Educational Progress in the areas of science and mathematics (Wenglinsky, 2000).

• Students have higher achievement rates when the focus of instruction is on meaningful conceptualization, especially when it emphasizes their own knowledge of the world (Donovan, Bransford, & Pellegrino, 1999; Good & McCaslin, 1992; National Research Council, 1999).

• Effective teachers recognize that no single instructional strategy can be used in all situations. Rather, they develop and call on a broad repertoire of approaches that have proven successful for them with students of varying abilities, backgrounds, and interests (Bain & Jacobs, 1990; Cotton, 2000; Darling-Hammond, 2001; Good & McCaslin, 1992; Molnar et al., 1999; Peart & Campbell, 1999; Pressley et al., 1998; Shulman, 1987).

Related Resources: Allington, 2002; Bain & Jacobs, 1990; Blair, 2000; Bloom, 1984; Brookhart & Loadman, 1992; Brophy & Good, 1986; Cawelti, 2004; Cotton, 1999, 2000; Covino & Iwanicki, 1996; Darling-Hammond, 2000, 2001; Donovan et al., 1999; Education USA Special Report, n.d.; Good & McCaslin, 1992; Hoff, 2003; Marzano et al., 1993; Mason, Schroeter, Combs, & Washington, 1992; Molnar et al., 1999; NASSP, 1997; Palmer, 1990; Peart & Campbell, 1999; Randall et al., 2003; Rosenshine & Stevens, 1986; Shellard & Protheroe, 2000; Shulman, 1987; Taylor et al., 1999; Tomlinson, 2000; Wang et al., 1993b; Wenglinsky, 2000; Zahorik et al., 2003.

Responding to the Range of Student Needs and Abilities in the Classroom

All good teachers recognize that classes don't learn, students do. Nonetheless, how best to differentiate instruction and individualize for the range of student needs and abilities in the classroom is an ongoing challenge. Effective teachers tend to recognize individual and group differences among their students and accommodate those differences in their instruction (Tomlinson, 2003). They adapt instruction to meet student needs, which requires careful assessment and planning for all students in the classroom, as well as the ability to select from a range of strategies to find the optimal match to the context (Cawelti, 2004; Tomlinson, 1999). More discussion on assessing student learning to meet the needs of students can be found in Chapter 6.

Successful teachers present information in such a way that the majority of the class is challenged, yet can be successful. They adapt the assignment to meet the needs of students who are either functioning higher or lower or who simply need the material presented differently. They also take the time to teach study and organizational skills to students to provide them with the learning tools that many of their peers instinctively acquire and use (Cotton, 2000).

The ability to improvise while teaching to meet the learning needs of all students is another sign of an effective teacher. Students of teachers who receive specialized training in working with a broad range of students, including culturally diverse students, gifted students, and students with special needs, perform (on average) more than one full grade level above their peers (Wenglinsky, 2000). These teachers understand and use "scaffolding" approaches to instruction that allow students to receive the help they need and to work at their own pace. For gifted learners, curriculum compacting can be used so that a student is able to master the objectives and move on to investigations and applications of greater interest to that student. In summary, effective teachers use all available resources, including the school content-area specialists, other students, students' siblings, parents, classroom volunteers, tutors, community members, and before- and after-school meeting times to meet the needs of students.

Studies of student achievement and of perceptions of teacher effectiveness have emphasized the importance of appropriate differentiation in instruction, including the following findings:

• Students are most engaged and achieve most successfully when instruction is appropriately suited to their achievement levels and needs (Covino & Iwanicki, 1996).

• Effective teachers use a variety of grouping strategies, including cooperative grouping, flexible grouping, and ability grouping with differentiation to support student learning (Brophy & Good, 1986; Molnar et al., 1999; Taylor et al., 1999; Walberg, 1984).

• One-on-one tutoring increases student achievement significantly (Bloom, 1984; Mason et al., 1992; Success for All Foundation, 1998) and is a defining feature of an effective teacher (Peart & Campbell, 1999).

• Instructional differentiation requires careful monitoring and assessment of student progress, as well as proper management of activities and behavior in the classroom; placing students into groups based on ability without tailoring instruction to the different groups is insufficient to support academic success (Education Review Office, 1998; Kulik & Kulik, 1992).

• Effective teachers know and understand their students as individuals in terms of their abilities, achievement, learning styles, and needs (Bain & Jacobs, 1990; Brookhart & Loadman, 1992) and give greater emphasis to individualization in their teaching (Molnar et al., 1999; Walberg, 1984; Wenglinsky, 2002).

• Studies of student achievement have demonstrated that effective teachers demonstrate effectiveness with the full range of student abilities in their classrooms (Allington, 2002; Wright, Horn, & Sanders, 1997).

Related Resources: Bain & Jacobs, 1990; Blair, 2000; Brookhart & Loadman, 1992; Brophy & Good, 1986; Cawelti, 2004; Cotton, 1999, 2000; Covino & Iwanicki, 1996; Darling-Hammond, 2000; Education Review Office, 1998; Johnson, 1997; Kulik & Kulik, 1992; Mitchell, 1998; Molnar et al., 1999; Shellard & Protheroe, 2000; Taylor et al., 1999; Tomlinson, 1999, 2003; Wenglinsky, 2000, 2002; Wright et al., 1997.

Communicating High Expectations to Students

A teacher's ability to give clear and focused explanations to students and to clarify expectations for achievement is an important aspect of effective instructional delivery. Effective teachers expect students to learn; they take the responsibility to make sure students *do* learn. They set high standards and ensure a challenging curriculum for all students. Although achievement is related to the range of teaching strategies a teacher employs, clarity of explanation and expectation is a separate skill that is also vital in teacher effectiveness.

Communication is fundamental to any profession that requires interaction among people and within an organization. Teaching is no exception. Clarity in explanation—an important communication skill—is manifested in two primary ways in the teaching process. The first relates to the teacher's ability to explain content clearly and in a focused manner, pointing out concepts and relationships. The second concerns the teacher's clarity in terms of explaining directions for how students are to complete an activity. Further, the teacher's job requires clear communication of expectations, encouragement, and caring. This communication extends both to students and to parents. Effective teachers inform parents of the expectations for student growth and communicate how students are assessed for improvement (Allington, 2002). Moreover, the communication of content in teaching is far more than relating information. Effective communication in teaching requires teachers to clearly understand subject matter and know how to share that subject matter with students in a way that they come to own it and understand it deeply (Education Review Office, 1998; Rowan, Chiang, & Miller, 1997).

Effective communication on the part of the teacher involves not only one-way communication from teacher to student, but also communication from student to teacher and student to student. Effective teachers respond to student questions and comments in a way that further develops positive relationships and fosters an atmosphere of high expectations within the classroom. They encourage dialogue in the classroom, both between teacher and student and between student and student (Mason et al., 1992; Molnar et al., 1999). Effective teachers facilitate open discussion within the classroom.

Because, in the eyes of students, the teacher's affective characteristics are often of primary concern, teachers must constantly communicate a climate of support and encouragement to ensure that students participate actively in the two-way teaching and learning process. Furthermore, effective management and student learning are clearly related to communicating expectations.

In several studies, teacher expectations and the ability to effectively communicate those expectations have been shown to relate to student achievement as follows:

• Students and teachers who are asked about teaching effectiveness consistently note the importance of clearly explaining the content (Emmer et al., 1980; NASSP, 1997; Peart & Campbell, 1999).

• Examples and guided practice (as appropriate to the lesson) are important parts of getting the point of the lesson across; additionally, these examples may represent clarity both in content and in directions and procedures (Covino & Iwanicki, 1996; Emmer et al., 1980; Good & McCaslin, 1992; Rosenshine & Stevens, 1986; Zahorik et al., 2003).

• Teachers can improve the performance of students who normally exhibit average achievement by setting and communicating high expectations (Mason et al., 1992; Walberg, 1984).

• Successful teachers cite high expectations for themselves and their students as a key part of their success (Covino & Iwanicki, 1996).

• Expectations that are set high represent an overall orientation toward improvement and growth in the classroom. High expectations have been demonstrated to be a defining characteristic of benchmark schools (Cotton, 2000).

• Teachers stress students' personal responsibility and accountability for striving to meet high expectations (Covino & Iwanicki, 1996), partially through an emphasis on improvement through the assessment model used (Allington, 2002). Linked to this emphasis is the importance of teaching students metacognitive strategies to support reflection on learning progress (Porter & Brophy, 1988).

• Effective teachers promote student self-regulation (Day, 2002; Porter & Brophy, 1988; Pressley et al., 1998).

Related Resources: Allington, 2002; Bain & Jacobs, 1990; Berliner & Rosenshine, 1977; Blair, 2000; Brophy & Good, 1986; Cawelti, 1999, 2004; Cotton, 1999, 2000; Covino & Iwanicki, 1996; Day, 2002; Demmon-Berger, 1986; Emmer et al., 1980; Good & Brophy, 1997; Good & McCaslin, 1992; Johnson, 1997; Marzano et al., 1993; Mason et al., 1992; NASSP, 1997; Peart & Campbell, 1999; Porter & Brophy, 1988; Pressley et al., 1998; Rosenshine & Stevens, 1986; Walberg, 1984; Wang et al., 1993b; Zahorik et al., 2003.

Understanding the Complexities of Teaching

Teaching occurs at a crossroads of complex disciplines and involves interacting with diverse and complex student learners. The effective teacher must have sufficient knowledge of subject matter and of teaching and learning to appreciate these complexities. An understanding of these complexities can help prevent the teacher from trivializing content and from underestimating the work it will take to prepare lessons and to implement them with students. The effective teacher also recognizes each student as a multifaceted person, understanding that each student brings a lifetime of ideas and experiences in and out of school to the classroom. Moreover, the effective teacher recognizes that a class is, itself, a dynamic and complex entity, made of many personalities, evolving into a corporate personality of its own. All these understandings contribute to a teacher's interactions with students, plans and practices for managing the environment, and preparation and differentiation for student learning needs. In a word, teaching is complex.

Unfortunately, teaching and learning does not always focus on both the memorization of material and the more complex tasks of applying, synthesizing, and evaluating. A review of the Third International Mathematics and Science Study (TIMSS) 1999 Video Study provides a case in point regarding the complexity of teaching (Hiebert et al., 2005). Researchers found that mathematics teachers in the United States focus learning on low-level content, routine exercises, and procedures that students had already learned. Mathematics students in the United States spent 34 percent of time per lesson applying what they had learned versus students in Japan, who spent 74 percent of their time in application. While procedures are a necessary part of learning mathematics, learning should not stop at that level. Effective teachers understand how to scaffold student learning from the simple to the complex.

Effective teachers emphasize meaning. They encourage students to respond to questions and activities that require them to discover and assimilate their own understanding, rather than to simply memorize material (Marzano et al., 1993). A study of 3rd and 8th graders found that students who received instruction that emphasized analytical, creative, and practical thinking performed better on assessments than students who received instruction that emphasized memorization or analytical thinking only (Sternberg, 2003). Eisner (2003/2004) explained that effective schools, and thus, effective teachers emphasize critical thinking, and they cultivate a propensity for applying critical thinking in order to make good judgments.

These teachers also present and engage students in content at various levels of complexity, using a broad range of objectives and activities and employing activities and questions that address higher and lower levels of cognitive complexity. They scaffold lessons to guide students in their emerging skill and knowledge acquisition through step-by-step instructions, modeling, and opportunities to apply new information and skills to novel situations (Zahorik et al., 2003).

Research on effective teaching has yielded the following results with regard to cognitive complexity of classroom tasks:

• Effective teachers are concerned with having students learn and demonstrate understanding of meanings rather than merely memorizing facts or events (Demmon-Berger, 1986; Marzano et al., 1993).

• Effective schools and effective teachers prioritize reading because it affects success in other content areas and overall achievement gains (Allington, 2002; Taylor et al., 1999).

• Students have higher achievement rates when the focus of instruction is on meaningful conceptualization, especially when it builds on and emphasizes their own knowledge of the world (Mason et al., 1992; Molnar et al., 1999; Wenglinsky, 2000).

• Effective teachers make greater use of interdisciplinary connections, connections across the curriculum, and integration of subject areas in their teaching (Molnar et al., 1999; Pressley et al., 1998).

Related Resources: Berliner & Rosenshine, 1977; Blair, 2000; Brophy & Good, 1986; Cawelti, 2004; Cotton, 2000; Demmon-Berger, 1986; Good & Brophy, 1997; Hiebert et al., 2005; Marzano et al., 1993; Molnar et al., 1999; Porter & Brophy, 1988; Shellard & Protheroe, 2000; Taylor et al., 1999; Wenglinsky, 2000; Zahorik et al., 2003.

Using Questioning Techniques

Questions and answers, from teachers to students and back again, represent much of the academic interaction that takes place in schools. This process supports student engagement in learning and a teacher's ability to monitor the learning process. Although effectiveness research supports the importance of questioning, the definitions of the kinds of questions that are most beneficial vary. What is clear, however, is that good questioning is definitely an important aspect of effective teaching.

Several studies have shown greater levels of student achievement relating to the teacher's use of lower-level, concrete questions, but other studies have supported the benefits of higher-level questions in encouraging student achievement (see, for example, Berliner & Rosenshine, 1977; Taylor et al., 1999). This variance in results suggests the importance of a variety of question types to meet student needs and support student learning. Several key points outlined by these studies about questioning are as follows:

• Questions are most valuable when students have an opportunity to respond—correctly or incorrectly—because responses encourage student engagement, demonstrate understanding or misconception, and further the discussion (Brophy & Good, 1986; Cawelti, 2004).

• The level of difficulty and cognitive level of questions should reflect the instructional objectives and desired learning outcomes (Cawelti, 2004).

• Questions should be considered carefully and prepared in advance of a lesson to ensure that they support the goals and emphasize the key points, along with maintaining appropriate levels of difficulty and complexity (Walsh & Sattes, 2005).

• When planning, implementing, and assessing lessons, questions should be considered as a sequence, not as isolated units (Walsh & Sattes, 2005).

• Studies indicate that questioning techniques are imperative for teachers who desire to increase their ability in assessing student learning (Covino & Iwanicki, 1996).

• Wait time is an important aspect of questioning; longer wait times have been related to higher student achievement and increased participation and student-to-student interaction in several studies. The amount of wait time, however, should also be considered in terms of maintaining student engagement and lesson momentum (Stahl, 1994; Tobin, 1980; Tobin & Capie, 1982). In general, one to three seconds is sufficient, depending on the question.

Related Resources: Berliner & Rosenshine, 1977; Brophy & Good, 1986; Cawelti, 2004; Cotton, 1999, 2000,; Covino & Iwanicki, 1996; Darling-Hammond, 2000; Rosenshine & Stevens, 1986; Stahl, 1994; Taylor et al., 1999; Tobin, 1980; Tobin & Capie, 1982; Walsh & Sattes, 2005; Wang et al., 1993a, 1993b.

Supporting Student Engagement in Learning

Along with the importance of time allocated to instruction by the teacher, the time the students spend on task, or engaged in the teaching and learning activity, is an important contributor to classroom success. To encourage student involvement in activities and lessons, effective teachers use varying strategies, including calling on students in random order, providing any necessary additional clarification and illustration, and finding something positive to say when students do respond or interact. One study indicated that more effective teachers typically used four or more instructional activities within a single instructional segment (Zahorik et al., 2003). Effective teachers also view high-interest lessons as necessary to student engagement. Also teachers who use positive reinforcement, praise students, and employ meaningful activities are more likely to actively engage students in learning.

Some research results related to student engagement in learning include the following:

• Student engagement with learning activities is supported by the teacher's attention to the momentum of the daily lesson, to appropriate questioning, and to clarity of explanation in terms of both content and directions (Brophy & Good, 1986; Cawelti, 2004).

• Students who perceive a positive classroom environment report being more engaged in school (Fullerton, 2002).

• Effective teachers engage students by matching the students' skill level to the task challenge level (Shernoff, Csikszentmihalyi, Schneider, & Shernoff, 2003).

• Effective teachers are accepting, supportive, and persistent in challenging and engaging students in all aspects of instruction (Cruickshank & Haefele, 2001; Johnson, 1997; Pressley et al., 1998).

• Effective teachers vary not only their own instructional strategies but also the types of assignments and activities given to students to support increased student engagement (Cotton, 2000; Johnson, 1997).

• Step-by-step directions for procedures to be followed in a given activity have been shown to be an important part of student success in activities, and they also encourage high levels of student engagement (Berliner & Rosenshine, 1977; Brophy & Good, 1986; Emmer et al., 1980).

• Student engagement is maximized when students engage in authentic activities related to the content under study (Cunningham & Allington, 1999; Weiss & Pasley, 2004); for example, in primary classrooms, effective teachers engage all students in a variety of reading and writing tasks throughout the day (Allington, 2002; Taylor et al., 1999).

Related Resources: Australian Council for Educational Research, 2002; Bloom, 1984; Brophy & Good, 1986; Cawelti, 2004; Cotton, 1999, 2000; Covino & Iwanicki, 1996; Cruickshank

& Haefele, 2001; Cunningham & Allington, 1999; Demmon-Berger, 1986; Doyle, 1986; Emmer et al., 1980; Good & Brophy, 1997; Johnson, 1997; Pressley et al., 1998; Shernoff et al., 2003; Wang et al., 1993a, 1993b; Weiss & Pasley, 2004; Zahorik et al., 2003.

Teachers of At-Risk Students: Implementing Instruction

As virtually all teachers know, the range of abilities and needs of students in a single classroom can be great. Further, the effective teacher knows how to respond to those needs and engage learners in the process. One way to engage students and to increase learning is to use a variety of instructional strategies, depending on factors such as prior knowledge of the students and the content and skills to be taught. At-risk students benefit from direct instruction, hands-on learning, simulations, inquiry, and other strategies that work well with the general population of students (Langer, 2001; Wenglinsky, 2002, 2004). It is the teacher's skills in implementing these strategies, however, that distinguishes the more effective from the less effective.

Teachers of at-risk students hold both high behavioral standards and high academic expectations for their students. They insist on students completing work and require students to redo the assignment if not done properly. A case in point regarding high expectations can be found in U.S. Department of Defense (DOD) schools. In DOD schools, 85 percent of African American students and 93 percent of Hispanic students reported that they believed their teachers held high expectations for them. In contrast, a U.S. national sample revealed that 52 percent of African American students and 53 percent of Hispanic students believed that their teachers had positive expectations of them (Bridglall & Gordon, 2003). It is interesting to note that at-risk students in DOD schools outperform at-risk students at similar public schools.

Questioning is an important instructional strategy for improving academic achievement of at-risk students in its own right. Effective teachers use higher-level questions, use questioning to clarify students' understandings, and provide wait time for students to reflect and respond. In contrast with these strategies, lower-achieving schools emphasize lower-level questioning through basic remedial activities (Bennett et al., 2004; Bradford, 1999).

Effective teachers of at-risk students engage students in the learning process. In addition to the adept use of questioning, teachers increase student engagement by making connections between the curriculum and real life (National Academy of Sciences, 2004) and by coaching and actively involving students in the lesson. Students are "on their toes," as diverting their eyes from their teacher's will not guarantee them a pass on participation (Bernard, 2003; Corbett & Wilson, 2002).

Studies related to effectively teaching at-risk students reveal the following:

• Schools in which students are achieving against the odds maintain a climate of high student expectations (Bridglall & Gordon, 2003; North Carolina Department of Public Instruction, 2000; Peart & Campbell, 1999).

• Teachers focus on understanding rather than isolated facts (National Academy of Sciences, 2004; Hamre & Pianta, 2005; Pogrow, 2005; Pressley et al., 2004; Wenglinsky, 2004).

• Effective teachers of at-risk students use a wide variety of instructional strategies to meet the range of needs in the classroom (Corbett & Wilson, 2002; Ilmer et al., 1997; Peart & Campbell, 1999).

• Teachers in schools where students performed better than in comparable schools were more likely to use a combination of direct instruction, simulated learning activities, and instruction integrated among content areas (Langer, 2001).

• The higher the level of questions used in the classroom, the more academic growth was experienced by at-risk students (Taylor et al., 2003).

• There is a positive correlation between high engagement and students' reading comprehension (Taylor et al., 2003).

• Modeling is positively related to student growth in writing (Taylor et al., 2003).

Related Resources: Bennett et al., 2004; Bernard, 2003; Bradford, 1999; Bridglall & Gordon, 2003; Corbett & Wilson, 2002; Hamre & Pianta, 2005; Ilmer et al., 1997; Langer, 2001; National Academy of Sciences, 2004; North Carolina Department of Public Instruction, 2000; Peart & Campbell, 1999; Pogrow, 2005; Pressley et al., 2004; Taylor et al., 2003; Wenglinsky, 2002, 2004.

Teachers of High-Ability Students: Implementing Instruction

One defining attribute of effective teachers of high-ability students is that they must be masters of multitasking during classroom time. They must also be skilled in implementing various strategies to accommodate the range of abilities found among gifted students. Teachers of gifted and talented students must be able to help them see larger patterns, understand abstractions, and focus on discovery learning. Thus, teachers of high-ability learners strive to develop a wide range of teaching strategies and use this wide range to meet the individual needs and learning styles of their students (Hunt & Seney, 2001; VanTassel-Baska & Little, 2003).

As with all students, the skill of questioning is useful and necessary in teaching gifted learners. Typically, but not exclusively, questioning in gifted classrooms focuses on higher-level learning. Skillfully employing questioning strategies in the classroom requires a deep knowledge of the content and of pedagogy (National Research Council, 2000). Additionally, teachers may ask other students for feedback to a student's response. They repeat students' answers in order to allow students to hear their own words, and they provide time for students to ponder, test hypotheses, and reformulate. They also encourage students to formulate their own questions about content. A review of research studies found that when students generate their own questioning, their understanding of the content is strengthened and they become more intrinsically motivated (Walsh & Sattes, 2005). Therefore, effective teachers of the gifted not only question students but build students' capacity to generate questions themselves.

Effective teachers of high-ability students recognize the complexities inherent in teaching this population. They know how to develop the competencies and curiosity that reside within each student. In order to achieve this sometimes daunting task, they must first discover each student's special abilities. Then, the teacher must skillfully match the students' abilities with tasks that are challenging enough to engage and motivate. In particular, the effective teacher of high-ability learners assists students in directing their own learning in order to develop skills in research, original investigations, and independent study (Feldhusen, 1991; Hansen & Feldhusen, 1994).

A review of research and literature reveals the following conclusions:

• Teachers of gifted students are able to match individual skills and task complexities, which in turn motivates and engages students in the learning process (Csikszentmihalyi et al., 1993). Therefore, they must know how to develop competencies within each student (Feldhusen, 1991; Holloway, 2003).

• Effective teachers of gifted students are skillful at pacing instruction (Heath, 1997; Renzulli, 1999; Silverman, 1995) and focus class discussion on in-depth analysis (Hansen & Feldhusen, 1994).

• Effective teachers of high-ability learners actively engage students through a variety of instructional activities (Renzulli, 1997), including direct and indirect instruction in which the teacher can both lead and facilitate students through the learning process (VanTassel-Baska & Little, 2003).

• Effective teachers of high-ability students ask higher-level questions and have high levels of student engagement and student participation during questioning (Ford & Trotman, 2001; Henderson, 1996; Hansen & Feldhusen, 1994; Silverman, 1995).

Related Resources: Csikszentmihalyi et al., 1993; Feldhusen, 1991; Ford & Trotman, 2001; Hansen & Feldhusen, 1994; Henderson, 1996; Holloway, 2003; Hunt & Seney, 2001; Maddux et al., 1985; National Research Council, 2000; Renzulli, 1997; Silverman, 1995; VanTassel-Baska & Little, 2003; Walsh & Sattes, 2005.

Figure 5.1
Key References for Implementing Instruction

Reference	Instructional Strategies	Adapting Instruction	Content and Expectations	Complexity	Questioning	Student Engagement	Teachers of At-Risk Students	Teachers of High-Ability Students
Allington, 2002	•		•					
Australian Council for Educational Research, 2002						•		
Bain & Jacobs, 1990	•	•	•					
Bennett et al., 2004	•				•		•	
Berliner & Rosenshine, 1977			•	•	•			
Bernard, 2003			•				•	
Blair, 2000	•	•	•	•				
Bloom, 1984	•					•		
Bridglall & Gordon, 2003			•				•	
Brookhart & Loadman, 1992	•	•						
Brophy & Good, 1986	•	•	•	•	•	•		
Cawelti, 1999			•		•			
Cawelti, 2004	•	•	•	•	•	•		
Corbett & Wilson, 2002			•				•	
Cotton, 1999	•	•	•		•			
Cotton, 2000	•	•	•	•	•	•		
Covino & Iwanicki, 1996	•	•	•		•	•		
Cruickshank & Haefele, 2001						•		
Csikszentmihalyi et al., 1993	•			•				•
Cunningham & Allington, 1999						•		
Darling-Hammond, 2000		•			•			
Darling-Hammond, 2001	•							
Day, 2002			•					
Demmon-Berger, 1986			•	•		•		
Doyle, 1986						•		

Reference	Instructional Strategies	Adapting Instruction	Content and Expectations	Complexity	Questioning	Student Engagement	Teachers of At-Risk Students	Teachers of High-Ability Students
ERS, 2000				•				
Education USA Special Report, n.d.	•							
Emmer et al., 1980			•			•		
Feldhusen, 1991	•			•			•	
Ford & Trotman, 2001					•	•		•
Good & Brophy, 1997			•			•		
Good & McCaslin, 1992	•		•					
Hamre & Pianta, 2005				•			•	
Hansen & Feldhusen, 1994	•			•				•
Heath, 1997	•							•
Hoff, 2003	•							
Holloway, 2003				•				•
Johnson, 1997	•	•	•			•		
Kulik & Kulik, 1992		•						
Langer, 2000, 2001	•						•	
Marzano et al., 1993	•		•	•				
Mason et al., 1992	•		•					
Mitchell, 1998		•						
Molnar et al., 1999	•	•	•					
NASSP, 1997			•					
Palmer, 1990	•							
Peart & Campbell, 1999	•		•				•	
Pogrow, 2005	•			•			•	
Porter & Brophy, 1988			•	•				
Price, 2000			•					
Randall et al., 2003	•							

Figure 5.1 *Continued*
Key References for Implementing Instruction

Figure 5.1 *Continued*
Key References for Implementing Instruction

Reference	Instructional Strategies	Adapting Instruction	Content and Expectations	Complexity	Questioning	Student Engagement	Teachers of At-Risk Students	Teachers of High-Ability Students
Renzulli, 1997	•							•
Rosenshine & Stevens, 1986	•		•		•			
Shellard & Protheroe, 2000		•		•				
Shernoff et al., 2003						•		
Shulman, 1987	•							
Silverman, 1995					•	•		•
Taylor et al., 1999				•				
Taylor et al., 2003					•	•	•	
Tobin, 1980					•			
Tobin & Capie, 1982					•			
Tomlinson, 1999		•						
Walsh & Sattes, 2005					•			
Wang et al., 1993a			•		•	•		
Wang et al., 1993b	•		•		•	•		
Weiss & Pasley, 2004						•		
Wenglinsky, 2000	•	•		•				
Wenglinsky, 2002	•	•						
Wenglinsky, 2004	•						•	
Wright et al., 1997		•						
Zahorik et al., 2003	•		•			•		

6

Monitoring Student Progress and Potential

Ella is truly a data diva. She teaches 8th grade English and continually keeps her finger on the pulse of her students' progress. At the beginning of the year she collects an initial writing sample that serves as a baseline for targeted improvements for each student. She gives the Degrees of Reading Power (DRP) test to students to get another baseline. Throughout the year, she is constantly reading, analyzing, and critiquing her students' work, as well as providing specific and timely feedback. Additionally, Ella empowers her students to be their own best critics as she shares with them how to assess the quality of their own work and provide constructive criticism to their peers. She regularly reviews, grades, and assesses her students' progress. Ella updates their writing portfolios and uses predictor tests to help her better prepare her students for the state tests. If success is measured by standardized tests, then Ella is successful, but as Ella says, the proof is in what students can do, not just in their test scores. Ella's students exit her classroom on the last day of school better writers and more observant readers who are able to clearly articulate their thoughts through writing and discussion.

Monitoring and assessing student development and work is a complex task. With an increasing number of states linking high-stakes testing to graduation requirements and implementing statewide testing programs in the lower grades, teachers feel pressure to prepare students to be successful on the tests by aligning their instruction with the state's standards. Even as teachers provide experiences for students to learn material, they must still check for individual student learning. There are a variety of means to teach content and just as many ways to monitor and assess understanding. Effective teachers employ all the tools at their disposal to make a positive impact on students, including the use of homework and feedback. Figure 6.1, at the end of the chapter, provides a list of key references to the elements that effective teachers use to monitor student progress and potential.

The Importance of Homework

The value of homework is often questioned today, especially when students participate in so many other activities outside school and when teachers become frustrated with the number of students who do not complete homework assignments. Homework, however, remains an important part of effective teaching when it is used as an extension of the classroom.

Studies have been conducted to assess the value of homework in terms of student achievement, yielding the finding that the amount of time spent on homework is an influential school-based factor contributing to student learning and student participation (Cawelti, 2004; Cotton, 2000; Coulter, 1985; Covino & Iwanicki, 1996). One study stated that the basic purposes of homework are practice, preparation, and elaboration (Coulter, 1985). Practice-based homework is the reinforcement of familiar concepts that need to be refined. Preparation-focused homework exposes a student to a concept that the class will study in-depth on the next school day or in the near future. And elaboration exercises facilitate the exploration of related concepts.

Before assigning any type of homework, however, effective teachers establish guidelines that include the following information:
- Purpose of the assignment.
- Amount of homework that will be assigned.
- Expectations for completing homework as well as consequences for not completing it.
- Types and amount of assistance from parents that are considered appropriate.

In addition to setting these guidelines, effective teachers clearly communicate them to their students and parents.

A partnership among school support programs, teacher, and parents forms a triangle with the student in the center. In the triad, the teacher and the parents have the greatest contact with the child. Still, effective teachers do not naively assume that parents will support their child doing homework; rather, they equip parents with the tools to make homework time successful (Battle-Bailey, 2003). The more a parent is involved in the student's academic learning, including homework, the more the student is motivated to achieve (Gonzalez, 2002). Teachers share homework tips like these to use with families:

  • Provide statements and inquiries that parents can use with their child; for example:

    • "I know you usually have a vocabulary test on Tuesdays. Have you studied for it?"
    • "What needs to be done tonight for homework?"

  • Provide clear directions and written explanations of the homework so that the family member and the student understand the assignment.

  • Encourage parents and caregivers to designate a well-lit space for homework.

  • Suggest that families establish a time to do the work or use the calendar to plan when the work can be done if schedules vary.

  • Assure parents and caregivers that the teacher wants to hear if the student needs lots of coaching from the family member.

When teachers give families concrete ideas of how to support their children, the home and school connection is strengthened and the homework experience is more productive.

The quality of homework assignments is a more important issue than quantity (Senge et al., 2000). Effective teachers often assign homework that does not necessarily involve a finished paper to be submitted by the student. Rather, they assign homework that provokes thought for subsequent use in class discussions or writing activities. In fact, some researchers suggest that homework assignments should empower students to learn. This empowerment takes place only if students actually complete the homework. Related to this point, effective teachers provide specific goals and guidelines for homework and allow students to meet those requirements in various creative ways, including performances, creative literature, videotapes, and posters (Brophy & Good, 1997; Marzano, Pickering, & Pollock, 2001). Thus, they use homework as a tool to assess the learning needs of the broad range of students within their classroom.

Perhaps most important, effective teachers not only assign homework, but also check and review it regularly. Students of teachers who spend more time dispensing homework as well as providing considerable supportive feedback make higher gains than students whose teachers fail to spend this time on homework (Coulter, 1985). Feedback on completed homework is particularly important. A teacher provides corrective feedback, commenting on work that fails to meet criteria for success. By using these types of feedback on a regular basis, teachers can help increase students' learning gains by as much as 30 percentile points on a standardized test in one year, as indicated by one study (Marzano, Pickering, & Pollock, 2001). Students of teachers who do not provide regular feedback on homework only realize a third of the gain made by students of teachers who give timely and informative feedback. After all, it is not the frequency or amount of homework that is most powerful; it is the *feedback* on the homework that matters.

Additional research-supported findings include the following keys to effective homework:

• Homework has positive effects on student achievement when it is clearly explained and related to the content under study in the classroom and to student capacity (Danielson, 2002; Marzano, Pickering, & Pollock, 2001).

• Homework is more effective in influencing student achievement when it is graded, commented on, and discussed in class (Marzano, Pickering, & Pollock, 2001). Based on a synthesis of studies, graded homework has a strong effect related to student achievement (Cawelti, 2004); the effect for graded homework is far greater than for homework that is assigned but not graded (Walberg, 1984).

• Effective teachers list homework as an important element in students' success (Covino & Iwanicki, 1996).

• Homework has more of an effect in upper grades (6–12) than in lower grades (Cooper, Lindsay, Nye, & Greathouse, 1998).

• The amount of homework that students complete and the amount of parental involvement in homework is positively correlated with student grades (Battle-Bailey, 2003; Cooper, Jackson, Nye, & Lindsay, 2001; Keith, Reimers, Fehrmann, Pottebaum, & Aubey, 1986).

• For every additional 30 minutes spent on homework a night, high school students may increase their grade point averages by half a point (Marzano, Pickering, & Pollock, 2001).

Related Resources: Battle-Bailey, 2003; Cawelti, 1999, 2004; Cooper et al., 2001; Cotton, 2000; Covino & Iwanicki, 1996; Danielson, 2002; Education USA Special Report, n.d.; Gonzalez, 2002; Keith et al., 1986; Marzano, Pickering, & Pollock, 2001; Senge et al., 2000; Walberg, 1984, 1994; Wenglinsky, 2000.

Providing Meaningful Feedback

Educators recognize the importance of feedback to students on their work (Johnson, 1997). Feedback is one of the most powerful modification techniques for increasing learning outcomes in students (Berliner & Rosenshine, 1977; Walberg, 1984). Effective teachers provide feedback in a timely manner and ensure that it relates specifically to the criteria of the task. Studies have found that the amount of time between the activity and the feedback has a critical effect on student achievement (see, for example, Bangert-Downs, Kulik, Kulik, & Morgan, 1991). In fact, the longer the delay in giving feedback, the less likely students will respond to the feedback and the less likely learning will be enhanced.

Effective teachers provide feedback that is primarily corrective (Black & William, 1998; Marzano, Pickering, & Pollock, 2001). They avoid simply indicating right or wrong answers, because this practice can actually have a negative impact on student learning. Instead, effective teachers provide specific explanations of what students are doing correctly, what they are not doing correctly, and how to fix it (Chappius & Stiggins, 2002). One study indicated that students completed higher-quality work when they were given corrective feedback related to the content of the assignment than students who were not given corrective feedback (Matsumura, Patthey-Chavez, Valeds, & Garnier, 2002).

Students need to learn how to critically examine their own work and to provide constructive criticism to others (Black, Harrison, Lee, Marshall, & William, 2004; Black & William, 1998; Chappius & Stiggins, 2002; Marzano, Pickering, & Pollock, 2001). In fact, effective teachers take the time to instruct students on how to perform constructive criticism. A useful tool for many teachers is a rubric in which students are provided the parameters of success before working on the assignment. Students can then assess their own work prior to submitting it to the teacher. Subsequently, the teacher can use the same rubric for feedback. Depending on the assignment, offering students an opportunity to incorporate the feedback and resubmit work for additional credit is a worthwhile venture that reinforces the value of revisions. Thus, the effective teacher builds the capacity for students to be able to think critically about their own work and the work of others.

Without doubt, feedback gained from oneself, one's peers, and the teacher enhances the learning process. Effective teachers use multiple approaches to monitor student progress. They constantly probe and collect information from the learners with whom they work in class. A variety of techniques, including mental notes, work samples, and feedback, can assist the teacher in creating improved, more meaningful instruction for the students.

Here are additional findings related to the ongoing assessment process and teacher feedback:

• Teachers in schools with high achievement rates use pre-assessments to support targeted teaching of skills important to learn for standardized tests, as well as to group students for reteaching (Cawelti, 2004).

• Students whose teachers hold high expectations when grading assignments perform better than students whose teachers have lower expectations. Student achievement decreases when the teacher "grades easy" (Bonesronning, 2004).

• Effective teachers plan and implement good monitoring strategies by targeting questions to the lesson objectives (Black & William, 1998).

• Effective teachers encourage students to monitor their own learning and progress (Wharton-McDonald et al., 1998).

• Effective teachers carefully choose the information sources they use for assessing learning needs (Cotton, 2000; Covino & Iwanicki, 1996).

• Effective teachers think through likely misconceptions that may occur during instruction and monitor students for signs of these misconceptions (Porter & Brophy, 1988).

• Clear, specific, and timely feedback given throughout the learning process supports student learning (Chappius & Stiggins, 2002; Cotton, 2000; Marzano, Norford, et al., 2001; Marzano, Pickering, & Pollock, 2001; Walberg, 1984).

• Effective teachers give feedback in a manner that is supportive and encouraging to students (Peart & Campbell, 1999).

• Effective teachers reteach material to students who did not achieve mastery (Brophy & Good, 1986; Cotton, 2000), and they offer tutoring for students who need or seek additional help (Mason et al., 1992).

Related Resources: Bangert-Downs et al., 1991; Berliner & Rosenshine, 1977; Black & William, 1998; Blair, 2000; Bonesronning, 2004; Brophy & Good, 1986; Cawelti, 2004; Chappius & Stiggins, 2002; Cotton, 2000; Covino & Iwanicki, 1996; Good & McCaslin, 1992; Johnson, 1997; Marzano, Pickering, & Pollock, 2001; Mason et al., 1992; Matsumara et al., 2002; Mendro, 1998; Mitchell, 1998; Peart & Campbell, 1999; Porter & Brophy, 1988; Rosenshine & Stevens, 1986; Wang et al., 1993a, 1993b; Wharton-McDonald et al., 1998.

Using Assessments to Meet Student Needs

Assessment is a central element of the teaching process. Assessment is used to determine the effectiveness of a lesson in terms of student learning and student engagement, to evaluate student progress, and as a basis for continuing instruction. A common element of high-performing schools is the focus on using assessment data to set instructional goals and adjust instruction at the school level (Cawelti, 2004; Heritage & Chen, 2005). The effective teacher uses assessment efficiently at the student level to monitor student progress and to plan further instruction (Mitchell, 1998). Assessments of various formats provide feedback to the teacher about what strategies are working, which students need more targeted assistance, and what content needs to be revisited.

Effective teachers not only assess student learning during and after instruction, but also assess student knowledge of content and skills to be taught prior to instruction (Chappius & Stiggins, 2002; Walberg, 1984). They realize that by diagnosing such student knowledge, they can adapt their instruction to meet the students where they are (Cawelti, 2004). We know that when teachers use diagnostic and prescriptive methods for assessing and teaching, student achievement can improve dramatically (Walberg, 1984). Adapting instruction based on assessment information is discussed in more depth in Chapter 5.

Effective teachers use a variety of assessment practices to monitor student learning, including formal and informal assessments and formative and summative assessments (Wiggins & McTighe, 1998). They monitor student progress informally through such techniques as scanning and circulating around the room or simply talking to individuals or small groups of students about specific tasks or activities. These teachers make notes about difficulties they observe and spend time thinking about how they can better reach students. More formal monitoring of student progress includes teacher-made or standardized tests, projects, and writing assignments. Furthermore, assessment of student learning is not limited to just the individual; these approaches can be applied to a group of students as well.

Successful teachers frequently use in-class tests (Black & William, 1998; Bloom, 1984; Rosenshine & Stevens, 1986). They understand how to interpret and use the information discerned from standardized and teacher-made achievement tests. A common practice is to count how many students incorrectly answer a question and then to analyze that question to determine if it was misleading or if the students did not learn the material. Teachers also look at the type of questions a student incorrectly answers and consider whether teaching test-taking skills can assist the student. Finally, teachers can group questions by the concept they are assessing to determine if the entire concept needs to be retaught with a different instructional approach. Effective teachers follow up their assessments with reteaching and enrichment as needed. In addition, effective teachers ensure that assessments are aligned not only with the curriculum but also with the actual instruction that takes place. The research related to the importance of using assessments to meet student needs is summarized below:

• Effective schools use assessments systematically for flexible grouping of students (Taylor et al., 1999).

• A synthesis of research on high-performing schools found that these schools focused on making decisions based on data not only at the district level, but also at the school and classroom levels as well (Cawelti, 2004).

• Case studies of five high-performing urban school districts revealed that these school districts focused on using data to make instructional decisions and training principals and teachers in how to use assessments for learning (Snipes, Doolittle, & Herlihy, 2002).

• A meta-analysis of research found that the use of assessments for diagnosing and adjusting instruction in order to meet individual student needs resulted in an increase in student achievement (Walberg, 1984).

Related Resources: Black & William, 1998; Bloom, 1984; Cawelti, 2004; Chappius & Stiggins, 2002; Heritage & Chen, 2005; Mitchell, 1998; Rosenshine & Stevens, 1986; Snipes et al., 2002; Taylor et al., 1999; Tomlinson, 1999; Walberg, 1984; Wiggins & McTighe, 1998.

Teachers of At-Risk Students: Monitoring Student Progress

Monitoring student learning and recognizing potential in students is an essential characteristic of the effective teacher of at-risk students (Manning & Baruth, 1995). Specifically, at-risk students benefit from teachers who use frequent and varied assessments to diagnose student learning and then change instruction to close the gap between where the student is now and where the student should be (Cawelti, 2004; Janisch & Johnson, 2003). Assessment must be accompanied by instructional change in order for the assessment to be meaningful. Consequently, successful teachers of at-risk students improve achievement by modifying instruction based on data (Armor et al., 1976).

Homework is an issue that is of great concern for teachers of at-risk students. Due to factors at home and at school, students may have substantial obstacles to completing homework. One study found that lower-ability learners performed better under supervised study conditions at school than when completing homework at home (Coulter, 1985). In a survey of parents of at-risk students, researchers found that the parents felt that homework was important but felt inadequate to help their children with the assignments (Drummond & Stipek, 2004). When parents do work at home with their students, achievement increases (Christenson & Sheridan, 2001; Ho Sui-Chu & Willms, 1996). Given these findings, it is essential that teachers work to communicate with parents regarding homework and even provide homework workshops for parents.

While at school, teachers must informally assess student understanding of concepts or skills taught in the classroom prior to sending students home to practice a new skill. If students leave the classroom without understanding, then homework is more difficult than it should be (Coulter, 1985). Consider a student who is learning to find locations on a map using longitude and latitude. The teacher teaches this skill and provides guided practice throughout the lesson. However, the teacher does not informally assess whether all students can, in fact, find locations on a map using coordinates. The teacher sends a worksheet home in which students must apply this skill. Unfortunately, two students were lost during instruction, but the teacher did not walk around and check student understanding during guided practice. These students are likely to experience frustration in completing the homework or may not even attempt the homework. The effective teacher prevents this disconnect by checking to make sure that students have an understanding of the concept or skill before assigning homework for additional practice.

Adapting instruction to meet student needs is also characteristic of an effective teacher. The National Academy of Sciences (2004) found that effective schools focus on individualizing instruction because they recognize that what might work with a majority of students might not work for all students. Effective teachers of at-risk students use informal and formal means of assessment in order to change instruction to meet individual needs. As a case in point, one study of five high-poverty Texas high schools revealed that these high schools increased student achievement by focusing on data use to modify instruction (Clubine, Knight, Schneider, & Smith, 2001).

Adaptation can include changing the content, the process, and the products of learning (Tomlinson, 1999). The effective teacher knows what to change, how to change it, and when to change it. And if the teacher feels inadequate to help a student, the teacher enlists the help of other professionals (Cawelti, 2004).

Effective teachers of at-risk students do the following:

• Provide verbal and written feedback to students (Hamre & Pianta, 2005; Singham, 2001) through comments on homework and quizzes, and discuss student errors and how to fix them (Lewis, 2001; Taylor et al., 2000).

• Plan homework and class work based on the individual abilities of students (National Academy of Sciences, 2004).

• Change instructional approaches to meet the needs of individual students (Armor et al., 1976; Fidler, 2002).

• Find ways to involve parents in homework (Coulter, 1985; Drummond & Stipek, 2004).

• Perform ongoing classroom assessment regularly to inform instructional decisions (National Academy of Sciences, 2004).

Related Resources: Armor et al., 1976; Cawelti, 2004; Clubine et al., 2001; Coulter, 1985; Drummond & Stipek, 2004; Fidler, 2002; Hamre & Pianta, 2005; Janisch & Johnson, 2003; Lewis, 2001; Manning & Baruth, 1995; National Academy of Sciences, 2004; Singham, 2001; Taylor et al., 2000; Tomlinson, 1999.

Teachers of High-Ability Students: Monitoring Student Progress

Effective teachers of high-ability learners are especially adept in diagnosing, interpreting, and adapting instructional practices to meet the individual needs of their students. Unfortunately, one study found that a majority of gifted students were not participating in differentiated instructional activities. Most written assignments focused on some type of review or drill-and-practice exercise (Westberg, Archambault, Dobyns, & Salvin, 1993). Additionally, a survey of middle school principals and teachers revealed that one-half of the teachers surveyed and one-third of the principals surveyed do not view differentiation as a need and identified time and resources as barriers to differentiating instruction (Tomlinson, Moon, & Callahan, 1998).

Tomlinson (2001) explained that differentiation of instruction is a way of thinking about teaching and learning, not merely a teaching strategy. It is the teacher's response to the needs of individual learners in the classroom in order to maximize student growth (Tomlinson & Allan, 2000). Effective teachers of gifted and talented students differentiate the content, process, and products of learning to meet student needs (Maker, 1982; Tomlinson, 1999). Furthermore, teachers of the gifted eliminate or de-emphasize previously learned material and use variable grouping strategies to enhance student learning (Starko & Schack, 1989). Ultimately, keys to differentiation are teacher flexibility, knowledge of students, and knowledge of instructional approaches.

Differentiated curriculum results in increased student understanding and in student learning gains. A study of a particular differentiated curriculum model, the Integrated Curriculum Model, revealed that students exposed to the program in social studies experienced significant gains in conceptual thinking, critical thinking, and learning content. Likewise, students exposed to the Integrated Curriculum Model in language arts showed significant gains in critical thinking and reading comprehension (VanTassel-Baska, 2005).

Feedback for instructional planning and for student understanding is another critical attribute of an effective teacher. However, feedback that is controlling in nature is counterproductive in the gifted classroom (Csikszentmihalyi et al., 1993). Rather, teachers who provide informational feedback that encourages student experimentation and suggestions for improvement motivate students to improve upon their own work (Bloom, 1985; Csikszentmihalyi et al., 1993).

Research and literature indicate that effective teachers of gifted students do the following:

• Individualize instruction in a way that addresses both individual and cultural differences (Ford & Trotman, 2001).

• Develop skills in differentiating curriculum for gifted learners (Feldhusen, 1991; Hansen & Feldhusen, 1994; Nelson & Prindle, 1992).

• Use feedback to structure lessons (Henderson, 1996) and increase student understanding (Bloom, 1985; Csikszentmihalyi et al., 1993).

• Use diagnostic tools to identify student abilities and talents (VanTassel-Baska, 1998).

Related Resources: Bloom, 1985; Csikszentmihalyi et al., 1993; Feldhusen, 1991; Ford & Trotman, 2001; Hansen & Feldhusen, 1994; Maker, 1982; Nelson & Prindle, 1992; Starko & Schack, 1989; Tomlinson, 2001; Tomlinson & Allan, 2000; Tomlinson et al., 1998; VanTassel-Baska, 1998, 2005; Westberg et al., 1993.

Figure 6.1
Key References for Monitoring Student Progress and Potential

Reference	Homework	Providing Meaningful Feedback	Using Assessment Information to Meet Student Needs	Teachers of At-Risk Students	Teachers of High-Ability Students
Armor et al., 1976			•	•	
Battle-Bailey, 2003	•				
Berliner & Rosenshine, 1977		•			
Black & William, 1998		•	•		
Black et al., 2004		•			
Blair, 2000					
Bloom, 1985		•			•
Bonesronning, 2004		•			
Brophy & Good, 1986		•			
Cawelti, 1999	•				
Cawelti, 2004	•	•	•	•	
Chappius & Stiggins, 2002		•	•		
Clubine et al., 2001			•	•	
Cooper et al., 1998	•				
Cooper et al., 2001	•				
Cotton, 2000		•			
Coulter, 1985	•			•	•
Covino & Iwanicki, 1996	•	•			
Csikszentmihalyi et al., 1993		•			•
Danielson, 2002	•				
Darling-Hammond, 2000					
Drummond & Stipek, 2004	•			•	
Education USA Special Report, n.d.	•				
Feldhusen, 1991					•
Fidler, 2002			•	•	

Figure 6.1 *Continued*					
Key References for Monitoring Student Progress and Potential					
Reference	Homework	Providing Meaningful Feedback	Using Assessment Information to Meet Student Needs	Teachers of At-Risk Students	Teachers of High-Ability Students
Ford & Trotman, 2001			•		•
Gonzalez, 2002	•				
Good & McCaslin, 1992		•			
Hamre & Pianta, 2005		•		•	
Hansen & Feldhusen, 1994			•		•
Henderson, 1996	•				•
Heritage & Chen, 2005			•		
Janisch & Johnson, 2003			•	•	
Johnson, 1997		•	•		
Keith et al., 1986	•				
Kulik & Kulik, 1992			•		
Lewis, 2001	•			•	
Maker, 1982			•		•
Manning & Baruth, 1995		•		•	
Marzano, Pickering, & Pollock, 2001		•			
Mason et al., 1992	•	•			
Matsumara et al., 2002		•			
Mendro, 1998		•			
Mitchell, 1998		•	•		
Molnar et al., 1999					
National Academy of Sciences, 2004	•	•		•	
Nelson & Prindle, 1992			•		•
Peart & Campbell, 1999		•			
Porter & Brophy, 1988		•			
Rosenshine & Stevens, 1986		•	•		

Figure 6.1 *Continued* **Key References for Monitoring Student Progress and Potential**					
Reference	**Homework**	**Providing Meaningful Feedback**	**Using Assessment Information to Meet Student Needs**	**Teachers of At-Risk Students**	**Teachers of High-Ability Students**
Senge et al., 2000	•				
Singham, 2001		•		•	
Snipes et al., 2002			•		
Starko & Schack, 1989			•		•
Taylor et al., 2000		•	•	•	
Tomlinson, 1999			•	•	•
Tomlinson, 2001			•	•	•
Tomlinson & Allan, 2000			•		•
VanTassel-Baska, 1998			•		•
VanTassel-Baska, 2005			•		•
Walberg, 1984	•				
Walberg, 1986	•				
Wang et al., 1993a		•			
Wang et al., 1993b		•			
Wenglinsky, 2000	•		•		
Wharton-McDonald et al., 1998		•			
Wiggins & McTighe, 1998			•		

7

Effective Teaching:
What Does It All Mean?

Think for a moment about your favorite teacher. Picture the teacher's appearance. Make a mental list of what made that teacher so special that years after leaving elementary school, middle school, high school, or college, you can still remember the teacher's name. Now, compare your mental list to what you have read in this book. How many effective teacher characteristics can you identify in your memory of your favorite teacher?

We are inherently drawn to teachers who are effective for us, whether we struggled with a particular concept and the teacher helped us to gain understanding, or whether we excelled in a particular area and the teacher challenged us to stretch our abilities. Those qualities still resonate with us years after leaving that effective teacher's classroom. In research and in real life, we cherish many portraits of effective teachers. We have been students of teachers, parents of students of teachers, and teachers, ourselves. As I hope is evident from this book and the research upon which it is based, as educators we have long searched for an answer to a fundamental question: What makes an effective teacher effective? Clearly, answers to this question are far from simple. Moreover, the answers are complex because the question is complex.

Effective teaching is the result of a combination of many factors, including aspects of the teacher's background and ways of interacting with others, as well as specific teaching practices. To discover what makes an effective teacher, we must understand what is meant by the word *effective*, realizing that the definition of this term has multiple layers and implications within the teaching profession. As Arthur Wise, president of the National Council for the Accreditation of Teacher Education (NCATE) noted, the fundamental purpose of teacher preparation programs is "preparing teachers who will be able to help all students learn, regardless of their socioeconomic status, race/ethnicity, and exceptionalities. The next generation of teachers must master multiple teaching strategies and must be able to adapt instruction to the students they serve" (personal communication, November 9, 2005). Moreover, Wise's description of teacher capacity holds true for the teaching profession in general.

Effective Teaching: A Summary

Based on the assumption that elements from all the categories identified in this book must be integrated to achieve teaching effectiveness, the research results included in *Qualities of Effective Teachers, 2nd edition* might be summarized under four overarching statements describing the effective teacher for students of all ability levels and backgrounds:

- The effective teacher *cares* deeply.
- The effective teacher recognizes *complexity*.
- The effective teacher *communicates* clearly.
- The effective teacher serves *conscientiously*.

Indeed, these "Four Cs" could be used to epitomize the teacher we aspire to be.

Caring Deeply

A central theme that resonates throughout the research and literature regarding effective teachers is that of a caring teacher. Students remember teachers who care about them by getting to know them as individuals and by getting to know their families and communities. The effective teacher seeks to understand the challenges facing their students by inquiring as to their well-being—whether that caring is evidenced in a simple phone call home when a child has missed a few days or a congratulatory note when a child has made an accomplishment. Additionally, the caring teacher recognizes that challenges at home affect a student's performance at school and works with the student and the family to overcome those challenges.

Caring does not, however, entail just a kind word, a phone call home, or a congratulatory note; caring also involves providing the support to help a child succeed and holding a child accountable for his or her own learning. What is the benefit of telling a child, "You can do it," when the child does not have the capacity to achieve? What is the benefit of expressing belief in a child's ability to accomplish a task without the support and expectation that the child will actually experience success? Thus, a caring teacher cares deeply enough to help make the verbal encouragement become reality.

Recognizing Complexity

Teaching is an extraordinarily complex undertaking. To illustrate, just think about how we teach a young child to read or an older student to understand algebraic equations. In either case, teaching—at least, successful teaching—incorporates conveying information about complex disciplines and processes to complex pupils. Teaching is the ability to transfer knowledge so that the learners acquire—even own—the knowledge and skills for themselves.

To succeed, the effective teacher must have sufficient knowledge of content, of pedagogy, of context, and of students to appreciate the intricacies that are bound up in the teaching and learning process. Whether the student experiences difficulties or is ready to move to the next level of understanding of a concept, the teacher must match the skill level of the student with the appropriate challenge. This deep understanding of complexity can help prevent the teacher from trivializing content and underestimating the work it takes to prepare lessons. An understanding of complexity is also reflected in the effort it takes to implement the lessons with students.

The effective teacher also recognizes each student as a unique individual, understanding that each one brings his or her own set of experiences and perspectives to the classroom. Moreover, the effective teacher recognizes that a class is a dynamic and multifaceted entity, made up of myriad personalities, with a personality all its own.

All these understandings contribute to a teacher's interactions with students, plans and practices for managing the environment, and preparation and differentiation for student learning needs. In a word, the effective teacher understands and can successfully navigate *complexity*.

Recognizing and understanding for a teacher is like getting into the driver's seat of a five-speed stick-shift automobile. The ineffective driver manages to get the car in gear, but cuts the engine off at every stop sign. The effective driver, like the effective teacher, adeptly and simultaneously handles multiple tasks and multiple meanings without losing sight of the goal of moving toward a specific destination.

Communicating Clearly

Communication is a key to success in any profession that requires interaction among people and within an organization. The teacher's job requires clear articulation of expectations, encouragement, and caring, as well as content knowledge. Moreover, communicating content in teaching is far more than just talking about objectives. Effective communication in teaching requires that a teacher have a clear understanding of the subject matter and of how to share that material with students in such a way that they come to own and understand it deeply. Beyond directly teaching content knowledge and skills, effective teachers also must be adept at facilitating students' own search for knowledge.

The teacher's affective characteristics are often a primary concern to the students. Therefore, the teacher must constantly communicate a climate of support and encouragement to ensure that students are engaged in the two-way teaching and learning process. Furthermore, effective management and student learning are clearly related to how expectations are communicated. Ultimately, being an effective communicator is about repackaging and delivering a message so that others can receive, respond, adapt, and use the information successfully. Consequently, in our profession, the art of teaching is virtually synonymous with communicating effectively.

Serving Conscientiously

The final overarching construct that emerges from the review of effective teaching research is the teacher's willingness to dedicate time and energy to the profession. Working hard is important, but even better is working both hard and smart.

The effective teacher is concerned with his or her own continuous learning process and reflects on all the elements of performance in an effort to continuously improve. Effective teachers connect their own improvement with the improvement of the school and the school district. Therefore, their professional contributions focus on their own teaching, the teaching and learning within the building, and the teaching and learning within the greater school community. The importance of conscientious reflection and involvement in all aspects of teaching cannot be overemphasized in defining the effective teacher. It isn't just what happens in the confines of the classroom that makes a teacher effective.

Improving Teacher Effectiveness

So where do we go from here? To improve teacher effectiveness, we need to consider all aspects of the profession—from preservice and inservice training to recruitment and retention of high-quality teachers.

Many behaviors and characteristics found in effective teachers can be cultivated among novices through awareness brought about by observing other teachers, receiving peer feedback, cultivating collegial relationships, and participating in lifelong learning experiences. For those already in the field, high-quality professional development activities are necessary tools for improving teacher effectiveness. These activities must be collegial, challenging, and socially oriented, because learning itself entails these characteristics. Additionally, professional development training must be tailored to the individual teachers within a particular school to support both the individual and organizational needs as they exist within a particular context. In essence, teacher effectiveness is not an end product; rather, it is an ongoing, deliberate process. Teacher success is a lifelong pursuit.

One Size Doesn't Fit All

The second edition of *Qualities of Effective Teachers* attempts to define the idea of teaching effectiveness by summarizing and organizing research results in these six major categories:

- Prerequisites of effective teaching
- The teacher as a person
- Classroom management and organization
- Planning and organizing for instruction
- Implementing instruction
- Monitoring student progress and potential

Specific elements within each of these categories have been found to be important in the work of effective teachers, as demonstrated through the research summaries within each chapter.

Clearly, a teacher's success is not based on any one element or any single source. Rather, teacher effectiveness draws on a multitude of skills and attributes in different combinations and in different contexts to produce the results that define the concept. For example, a teacher whose effectiveness is marked by the use of a range of teaching strategies likely has had solid educational preparation through coursework and professional development. A teacher of at-risk students who is able to accurately diagnose potential challenges and opportunities within each student has a firm grounding in the role assessment plays in the learning process. Likewise, a teacher of gifted and talented students who administers pre-assessments for learning recognizes that a child has already mastered the material, and the teacher then differentiates instruction for that student. Additionally, these teachers can employ effective instructional strategies to address the range of student learning needs because of their training, development, and actual experience in using and reflecting on a range of teaching strategies.

Part of an effective teacher's good rapport with students is based on maintaining appropriate roles, which suggests clarity in behavioral expectations and consistency in response to disciplinary situations. Thus, the effective teacher demonstrates behaviors and characteristics related to all six major categories delineated in this book to achieve his or her goal of promoting a positive classroom climate and student learning. Nonetheless, while *Qualities of Effective Teachers,* 2nd edition, seeks to provide practical, insightful guidance regarding effective teaching, a critically important point should not be lost: one size does *not* fit all teachers.

There is no single formula for classroom success. We can identify attributes, background characteristics, and behaviors that contribute to success, but these are, in the final analysis, a general guide and not a prescription. Each teacher—in each unique classroom, in a personal and unique way—must continuously strive to achieve.

Effective Teaching: The Ultimate Proof

In one study of effective teaching, school board members, principals, and teachers were asked to answer the question, "What is the makeup of an effective teacher?" Each group focused on what was important from their respective viewpoints, and they concurred on three important points:

• Knowledge and caring are important effectiveness attributes.

• Communication and classroom management are vital to the success of teaching.

• Process and mastery are important products of teaching (Johnson, 1997).

What these school board members, administrators, and teachers were saying is that teachers' backgrounds and teaching processes are important; however, those characteristics, alone, are not enough to define effective teaching. The ultimate proof of teacher effectiveness is student results.

The ability to identify effective teachers and to cultivate effective teaching results in students gaining more during the time spent in the classroom. If a student walks through a teacher's classroom 180 or 190 times, that student should be better in a tangible, measurable way for the experience. The student should be able to read better, understand math more deeply, demonstrate a better understanding of his or her place in the world, or show other worthy achievements. In other words, measuring teacher success merely by teaching processes is not enough; outcomes count.

Simply put, *teacher success = student success*. The one clear, abiding hallmark of effective teaching is student learning. As Joe Carroll, a former teacher and educational researcher, so aptly stated, "nothing, absolutely nothing has happened in education until it has happened to a student" (1994, p. 87).

Reflecting back on the outstanding teacher you thought of at the beginning of the chapter, think about how that teacher was able to meet your learning needs within the classroom. Recall how you felt that knowing the teacher cared about you and your success. Consider how the teacher communicated in such a way that the concepts made sense. Now imagine what it took for that favorite teacher to create a positive experience in which you were challenged to achieve. That is an effective teacher!

Part 2

Teacher Effectiveness: Resources You Can Use

Part 2 of *Qualities of Effective Teachers, 2nd edition* contains resources that can be used to apply the content and concepts presented in Part 1. Divided into three major sections, Part 2 provides skills checklists, detailed lists of teacher responsibilities and associated teacher behaviors, and an annotated bibliography.

• • •

Section I: Teacher Skills Assessment Checklists

The Teacher Skills Assessment Checklists are based on a synthesis of the research presented throughout this book. The checklists are designed to identify key indicators of effectiveness in a teacher's practice. Each effectiveness quality identified in a checklist includes multiple indicators of success. The checklists also provide a continuum for rating relative strengths and weaknesses, ranging from ineffective to master.

Teachers can use the checklists for self-assessment and reviewing and reflecting on the components identified as important for effective teaching. Additionally, supervisors and peers can use the skills checklists in their assessment of another teacher's ability. The checklists are intended to identify strengths and weaknesses so that professional growth can be stimulated and professional development opportunities can be tailored to specific teacher needs.

Section II: Teacher Responsibilities and Teacher Behaviors

The information in this section is designed primarily to assist administrators and peer coaches in identifying key components of effectiveness as they visit classrooms and observe teachers in action. In essence, Section II is intended to facilitate a type of action that is focused on the behaviors teachers exhibit in their daily work. For some teachers, the guidance that can emerge from feedback on these classroom qualities may be the impetus to refine a strategy or add something new to their toolkit of skills and techniques.

Section III: Annotated Bibliography

For the reader who would like to know more about specific aspects of teacher effectiveness research, a selection of noteworthy resources are summarized in an annotated format. The short annotations are presented in a straightforward, compact, and uniform format for ease in referring to and using the information. The matrix preceding the annotated bibliography is a reference designed to connect the annotations with Chapters 1–6 of the book. Additionally, a complete list of all references used in *Qualities of Effective Teachers, 2nd edition* is provided at the end of Part 2.

Section I

Teacher Skills Assessment Checklists

Key to the Teacher Skills Checklists

Master: The teacher exhibits the quality such that others would be able to use him or her as an expert for how to work with students. The teacher not only has a sense of the quality, but demonstrates an understanding of the essence of the quality.

Professional: The teacher exhibits the quality most of the time.

Apprentice: The teacher demonstrates the quality to the degree necessary to make the classroom function. The teacher may lack fluidity of use, but the result is still effective.

Ineffective: The teacher would benefit from more work on the quality in terms of working with a teacher at the professional or master level, or taking classes.

Not Observed: The observer has not seen evidence of the quality, either through demonstration or observation.

Checklist 1—Teacher Skills Checklist **The Teacher as a Person**		Not Observed	Ineffective	Apprentice	Professional	Master
Quality	**Indicators**					
Caring	Exhibits active listening.					
	Shows concern for students' emotional and physical well-being.					
	Displays interest in and concern about the students' lives outside school.					
	Creates a supportive and warm classroom climate.					
Shows Fairness and Respect	Responds to misbehavior on an individual level.					
	Prevents situations in which a student loses peer respect.					
	Treats students equally.					
	Creates situations for all students to succeed.					
	Shows respect to all students.					
Interactions with Students	Maintains professional role while being friendly.					
	Gives students responsibility.					
	Knows students' interests both in and out of school.					
	Values what students say.					
	Interacts in a fun, playful manner; jokes when appropriate.					
Enthusiasm	Shows joy for the content material.					
	Takes pleasure in teaching.					
	Demonstrates involvement in learning activities outside school.					
Motivation	Maintains high-quality work.					
	Returns student work in a timely manner.					
	Provides students with meaningful feedback.					
Dedication to Teaching	Possesses a positive attitude about life and teaching.					
	Spends time outside of school to prepare.					
	Participates in collegial activities.					
	Accepts responsibility for student outcomes.					
	Seeks professional development.					
	Finds, implements, and shares new instructional strategies.					

Checklist 1—Teacher Skills Checklist (contd) **The Teacher as a Person**		Not Observed	Ineffective	Apprentice	Professional	Master
Quality	**Indicators**					
Reflective Practice	Knows areas of personal strengths and weaknesses.					
	Uses reflection to improve teaching.					
	Sets high expectations for personal classroom performance.					
	Demonstrates high efficacy.					

Checklist 2—Teacher Skills Checklist **Classroom Management and Organization**		Not Observed	Ineffective	Apprentice	Professional	Master
Quality	**Indicators**					
Classroom Management	Uses consistent and proactive discipline.					
	Establishes routines for all daily tasks and needs.					
	Orchestrates smooth transitions and continuity of classroom momentum.					
	Balances variety and challenge in student activities.					
	Multitasks.					
	Is aware of all activities in the classroom.					
	Anticipates potential problems.					
	Uses space, proximity, or movement around the classroom for nearness to trouble spots and to encourage attention.					
Organization	Handles routine tasks promptly, efficiently, and consistently.					
	Prepares materials in advance and has them ready to use.					
	Organizes classroom space efficiently.					
Discipline of Students	Interprets and responds to inappropriate behavior promptly.					
	Implements rules of behavior fairly and consistently.					
	Reinforces and reiterates expectations for positive behavior.					
	Uses appropriate disciplinary measures.					

Checklist 3—Teacher Skills Checklist **Planning and Organizing for Instruction**		Not Observed	Ineffective	Apprentice	Professional	Master
Quality	**Indicators**					
Importance of Instruction	Focuses classroom time on teaching and learning.					
	Links instruction to students' real-life situations.					
Time Allocation	Follows a consistent schedule and maintains procedures and routines.					
	Handles administrative tasks quickly and efficiently.					
	Prepares materials in advance.					
	Maintains momentum within and across lessons.					
	Limits disruption and interruptions.					
Teachers' Expectations	Sets clearly articulated high expectations for self and students.					
	Orients the classroom experience toward improvement and growth.					
	Stresses student responsibility and accountability.					
Instruction Plans	Carefully links learning objectives and activities.					
	Organizes content for effective presentation.					
	Explores student understanding by asking questions.					
	Considers student attention span and learning styles when designing lessons.					
	Develops objectives, questions, and activities that reflect higher- and lower-level cognitive skills as appropriate for the content and the students.					

Checklist 4—Teacher Skills Checklist **Implementing Instruction**		Not Observed	Ineffective	Apprentice	Professional	Master
Quality	**Indicators**					
Instructional Strategies	Employs different techniques and instructional strategies, such as hands-on learning.					
	Stresses meaningful conceptualization, emphasizing the students' own knowledge of the world.					
	Suits instruction to students' achievement levels and needs.					
	Uses a variety of grouping strategies.					
Content and Expectations	Sets overall high expectations for improvement and growth in the classroom.					
	Gives clear examples and offers guided practice.					
	Stresses student responsibility and accountability in meeting expectations.					
	Teaches metacognitive strategies to support reflection on learning progress.					
Complexity	Is concerned with having students learn and demonstrate understanding of meaning rather than memorization.					
	Holds reading as a priority.					
	Stresses meaningful conceptualization, emphasizing the students' knowledge of the world.					
	Emphasizes higher-order thinking skills in math.					
Questioning	Asks questions that reflect type of content and goals of the lesson.					
	Varies question type to maintain interest and momentum.					
	Prepares questions in advance.					
	Uses wait time during questioning.					
Student Engagement	Is attentive to lesson momentum, appropriate questioning, and clarity of explanation.					
	Varies instructional strategies, types of assignments, and activities.					
	Leads, directs, and paces student activities.					

Checklist 5—Teacher Skills Checklist						
Monitoring Student Progress and Potential						
Quality	**Indicators**	Not Observed	Ineffective	Apprentice	Professional	Master
Homework	Clearly explains homework.					
	Relates homework to the content under study and to student capacity.					
	Grades, comments on, and discusses homework in class.					
Monitoring Student Progress	Targets questions to lesson objectives.					
	Thinks through likely misconceptions that may occur during instruction and monitors students for these misconceptions.					
	Gives clear, specific, and timely feedback.					
	Reteaches students who did not achieve mastery and offers tutoring to students who seek additional help.					
Responding to Student Needs and Abilities	Monitors and assesses student progress.					
	Uses data to make instructional decisions.					
	Knows and understands students as individuals in terms of ability, achievement, learning styles, and needs.					

Teacher Responsibilities and Teacher Behaviors

The positive and negative behaviors exhibited by teachers determine to a great extent their effectiveness in the classroom and, ultimately, the impact they have on student achievement. Several specific characteristics of teacher responsibilities and teacher behaviors that contribute directly to effective teaching are listed for each of the following categories:

- The teacher as a person
- Classroom management and organization
- Planning and organizing for instruction
- Implementing instruction
- Monitoring student progress and potential
- Professionalism

Red flags signaling ineffective teaching are presented at the end of each section. Both positive and negative characteristics are based on a plethora of research-based studies that address the concept of improving the educational system for both students and teachers. These qualities are general for any content area or grade level. Subject-specific qualities presented for the four content areas typically found in all schools include English, history and social studies, mathematics, and science. These lists are provided as a vehicle to promote teacher effectiveness.

The Teacher as a Person

Teachers are the representatives of both their content areas and their schools. How teachers present themselves makes an impression on administrators, colleagues, parents, and students. Often a student links the preference for a particular subject to a teacher and the way the subject was taught. A teacher who exudes enthusiasm and competence for a content area may transfer those feelings to the students. In addition, how the teacher relates to the pupils has an impact on the students' experience in the class. The teacher's personality is one of the first sets of characteristics to look for in an effective teacher. Many aspects of effective teaching can be cultivated, but it is difficult to effect change in an individual's personality.

Positive Qualities

- Assumes ownership for the classroom and students' success
- Uses personal experiences to provide real-world examples in teaching
- Understands students' feelings
- Admits mistakes and corrects them immediately
- Thinks about and reflects on practice
- Displays a sense of humor
- Dresses appropriately for the position
- Maintains confidential trust and respect
- Is structured, yet flexible and spontaneous
- Is responsive to situations and students' needs
- Enjoys teaching and expects students to enjoy learning
- Finds the win-win solution in conflict situations
- Listens attentively to student questions, comments, and concerns
- Responds to students with respect, even in difficult situations
- Communicates high expectations consistently
- Conducts one-on-one conversations with students
- Treats students equally and fairly
- Engages in positive dialogue and interaction with students outside the classroom
- Invests time with single students or small groups of students outside the classroom
- Maintains a professional manner at all times
- Addresses students by name
- Speaks in an appropriate tone and volume
- Works actively with students
- Provides tutoring to students before and after school

Red Flags of Ineffective Teaching

- Believes that teaching is just a job
- Arrives late to school and class on a regular basis
- Has numerous classroom discipline problems
- Is not sensitive to a student's culture or heritage
- Expresses bias (positive or negative) with regard to students
- Works on paperwork during class rather than working with students
- Has parents complaining about what is going on in the classroom
- Uses inappropriate language
- Demeans or ridicules students
- Exhibits defensive behavior for no apparent reason
- Is confrontational with students
- Lacks conflict resolution skills
- Does not accept responsibility for what occurs in the classroom
- Fails to acknowledge student and parent concerns

Classroom Management and Organization

A classroom reveals telltale signs of its user's style. Typically, a well-ordered classroom has various instructional organizers, such as rules posted on walls. Books and supplies are arranged so that frequently needed ones are easily accessible. The furniture arrangement and classroom displays often reveal how the teacher uses the space. Once the students enter, the details of a classroom at work are evident. The teacher's plan for the environment, related to the organization of both the classroom and the students, allows the classroom to run itself amid the buzz of student and teacher interaction.

Positive Qualities

- Establishes instructional and noninstructional procedures starting on the first day of school
- Positions chairs in groups or around tables to promote interaction
- Manages classroom procedures to facilitate smooth transitions, instructional groups, procurement of materials and supplies, and supervision of volunteers and paraprofessionals in the classroom
- Manages student behavior through clear expectations and firm and consistent responses to student actions

• Maintains a physical environment where instructional materials and equipment are in good repair

• Covers walls with student work, student-made signs, memos, and calendars of student events

• Has students welcome visitors and observers and explain activities to them

• Emphasizes students addressing one another in a positive and respectful manner

• Encourages interactions and allows low hum of conversations about activities or tasks

• Maximizes the physical aspect of the environment

• Arranges classroom so that all students can see and hear instruction

• Provides easy access to instructional materials

• Manages emergency situations as they occur

• Maintains acceptable personal work space

• Establishes procedures for running the classroom and handling routine student needs (e.g., bathroom visits, pencil sharpening, throwing away trash)

• Provides positive reinforcement and specific, timely feedback

• Notes positive interactions among students

• Disciplines students with dignity and respect

• Shows evidence of established student routines for responsibilities and student leadership

• Exhibits consistency and fairness in management style

• Uses proximity to students to manage behavior

• Involves students in formulating classroom rules

• Posts classroom and school rules

• Posts appropriate safety procedures

Red Flags of Ineffective Teaching

• Arranges desks and chairs in rows facing forward (without regrouping)

• Displays inconsistencies in enforcing class, school, and district rules

• Is not prepared with responses to common issues (e.g., bathroom visits, pencil sharpening, disruptions)

• Uses strictly commercial posters to decorate walls

• Lists teacher-formulated rules and consequences for negative behaviors

• Emphasizes facts and correct answers

- Gives unclear directions or explanations
- Punishes the entire class for the behavior of a few students
- Confronts student behavior in front of the entire class
- Assigns one task to be completed by all students
- Does not post or is not clear about expectations of students
- Does not display school or classroom rules
- Allows student disengagement from learning
- Is unavailable outside of class for students
- Complains inappropriately about administrative details
- Maintains an unsafe environment or equipment
- Fails to provide students with specific routines or responsibilities
- Keeps an unclean or disorderly classroom
- Uses many discipline referrals
- Makes up rules and consequences or punishment according to mood; is unpredictable
- Does not start class immediately; takes roll and dallies

Planning and Organizing for Instruction

Some teachers plan at home, and others work after school, crafting unit plans that incorporate various objectives. Regardless of where or how teachers plan and organize for instruction, the evidence of effective work is seen in the classroom. An observer in the classroom of an effective teacher can quickly comprehend the teacher's work by viewing the daily lesson objectives and activities posted. Further, the teacher is able to share what the class will be doing to follow-up on the lesson of the day. In many schools, teachers are required to submit weekly lesson plans; these plans typically note accommodations for different learning styles or needs and the variety of instructional approaches that will be used. It is important to note, however, that a lesson plan is not a final product; it is merely a description of what should be occurring in the classroom. Thus, a good plan doesn't guarantee high-quality instruction, but a poor plan most certainly contributes to ineffective instruction.

Positive Qualities

- Writes lesson plans for every school day
- Develops a syllabus to serve as a blueprint for the school year

- Gives students an agenda of objectives and activities so that they know the daily plan
- Uses student assessment and diagnostic data in instructional planning
- Includes assessment data and pretest results in the preparation of lesson plans
- Considers student work samples when writing lesson plans
- Aligns lesson plans with school district curriculum guides
- Creates teacher-developed assessments that promote higher-order thinking skills and are aligned with curriculum guides
- Incorporates state learning objectives into the lesson plans
- Writes lesson plans with clearly stated objectives that have measurable outcomes
- Includes use of available materials in lesson plans
- Incorporates technology in lesson plans
- Integrates other content areas when appropriate
- Indicates start and ending times for activities in lesson plans
- Includes activities and strategies to engage students of various ability levels in lesson plans
- Writes lesson plans that address review of materials or remediation and enrichment
- Incorporates effective questioning into lesson plans
- Addresses different learning modalities and styles in lesson plans
- Includes required accommodations for students with special needs in lesson plans
- Develops lesson plans that anticipate student misconceptions and prior knowledge and identifies strategies for addressing these
- Posts state standards or essential questions in classroom
- Provides pacing information in lesson plans
- Makes lesson plans for a substitute or an emergency that contain all necessary information available in an easily accessible area of the classroom

Red Flags of Ineffective Teaching

- Uses no (or very few) lesson plans or plans that are poorly written
- Does not have student assessment and diagnostic data available
- Makes no connection between assessment data and instructional planning

- Does not provide differentiated instruction
- Uses the textbook as the primary tool for planning
- Does not align lesson plans with local or district curriculum guides
- Does not incorporate state learning objectives into lesson plans
- Selects activities that are unrelated to the learning objective
- Teaches content that is inaccurate
- Develops lessons that are too difficult or too easy for the grade level
- Does not plan for or anticipate potential problems
- Writes lesson plans that mainly consist of text, lecture, or worksheets
- Does not actively engage students in learning
- Fails to address different learning styles or modalities of students in lesson plans
- Does not make accommodations for students with special needs in lesson plans
- Fails to post state standards or essential questions in the classroom
- Develops lesson plans in which information on pacing is not discernible
- Creates lesson plans that are disjointed
- Writes lesson plans that are sketchy and do not allow for smooth transitions between activities
- Shows a prevalent pattern of poor or inconsistent student achievement
- Does not provide emergency lesson plans
- Does not provide materials for substitutes (e.g., attendance rolls, class procedures, lesson plans, fire and tornado drill evacuation route maps)

Implementing Instruction

Effective teaching combines the essence of good classroom management, organization, effective planning, and the teacher's personal characteristics. The classroom presentation of the material to the students and the provision of experiences for the students to make authentic connections to the material are vital. The effective teacher facilitates the classroom similar to how a symphony conductor brings out the best performance from each musician to make a beautiful sound. In the case of the classroom, each student is achieving instructional goals in a positive classroom environment that is supportive, challenging, and nurturing of those goals. The best lesson plan is of little use if the classroom management component is lacking or the teacher lacks rapport with the students. Implementing instruction is like opening night at the theater, where all the behind-the-scenes work is hidden and only the magic is seen by the audience. Effective teachers seem to achieve classroom magic effortlessly. The trained observer, on the other hand, is likely to feel great empathy and appreciation for the carefully orchestrated art of teaching.

Positive Qualities

- Uses students' questions and prior knowledge to guide the lesson
- Responds spontaneously to student questions
- Helps students to make real-world connections to the content
- Delivers instruction in a logical, sequential manner
- Uses pre-assessments to guide instruction
- Makes subject matter relevant to students
- Develops elements of an effective lesson
- Uses established procedures to capture more class time (e.g., students have roles to play, such as passing out materials so that the teacher doesn't need to stop the momentum of the lesson)
- Incorporates higher-order thinking strategies
- Uses a variety of activities and methods to actively engage students
- Monitors student engagement in all activities and strategies
- Continuously has high numbers of students on task
- Adjusts the delivery and pacing of the lesson in response to student cues
- Effectively uses the entire classroom (e.g., moves throughout the room)
- Plans for student-centered classroom rather than teacher-centered classroom
- Provides specific feedback (verbal, nonverbal, written)
- Designs and bases assignments on measurable objectives
- Assists students in planning for homework assignments
- Makes changes to instruction throughout the lesson based on student feedback
- Encourages student-to-student and student-to-teacher interaction throughout the lesson
- Provides opportunities for review and practice
- Focuses learning at the beginning of the class time
- Provides closure at the end of the class time
- Models learning for students

Red Flags of Ineffective Teaching

- Consistently experiences student behavior problems
- Has unengaged students (bored, off-task, asleep)
- Has poor student performance in class and on assessments
- Gives vague instructions for seatwork, projects, and activities
- Fumbles through subject matter during instruction
- Is unresponsive to student cues that the delivery of instruction is ineffective
- Lacks variety in instructional methods used
- Has difficulty individualizing instruction
- Fails to incorporate technology
- Overuses paper and pencil tasks
- Uses outdated material or terminology
- Fails to implement needed changes pointed out by peers or supervisors
- Tells students to "know the material"
- Does not apply current research-based strategies or best practices
- Uses improper English
- Transitions slowly between activities or lessons
- Interacts very little with students during instruction
- Provides little time for students to interact with each other during the lesson
- Is unprepared to begin the lesson at the beginning of class or during transitions
- Pacing of the lesson is either too slow or too fast, not taking into account the developmental and ability levels of students
- Does not state or clarify the objective during the lesson
- Does not summarize learning at the end of the lesson

Monitoring Student Progress and Potential

Effective teachers have a sense of how each student is doing in the classes that they teach. They use a variety of formal and informal measures to monitor and assess their pupils' mastery of a concept or skill. When a student is having difficulty, the teacher targets the knowledge or skill that is troubling the student and provides remediation as necessary to fill in that gap. Communication with all parties vested in the success of the student is important, as parents and instructional teams are also interested in monitoring the student's progress. Monitoring student progress and potential need not be solely the responsibility of the teacher; indeed, an effective teacher facilitates students' understanding of how to assess their own performance. Ultimate accountability, however, does lie with each teacher, so students' progress and performance needs to be documented. An effective teacher who has observed and worked with a student has a sense of the potential that student possesses, encourages the student to excel, and provides the encouragement to motivate the student to make a sustained effort when needed.

Positive Qualities

- Provides methods for students to track their own performances
- Grades homework
- Gives specific oral and written feedback
- Documents student progress and achievement over time
- Makes instructional decisions based on student achievement data analysis
- Circulates in the room to assist students and provide praise
- Gives pre-tests and post-tests and graphs results
- Considers multiple assessments to determine whether a student has mastered a skill
- Keeps a log of parent communication
- Uses student intervention plans and maintains records of the plans' implementation
- Records team conference or teacher conference with students
- Gives informal and formal assessments on a regular basis
- Makes use of a variety of assessments
- Provides a description of record-keeping system and how it is used to inform parents, students, and administrators
- Provides assessment data that are both accurate and current
- Provides time and ways for students to self-assess
- Designs assessments to assess both higher- and lower-level content and skills
- Provides progress reports in a timely manner
- Uses rubrics or scoring guides for student assignments, products, and projects

- Practices differentiated instruction based on assessment analysis
- Exercises testing accommodations for students with special needs
- Maintains copies of all correspondence (written, e-mail, phone log) concerning student progress
- Holds teacher-parent-student conferences and meetings
- Produces class newsletters
- Invites parents and guests to special class events
- Maintains class Web page featuring student work and homework assignments
- Communicates using informal progress reports
- Uses appropriate and clear language in communications
- Participates in Individualized Education Program (IEP) meetings for students with special needs

Red Flags of Ineffective Teaching

- Does not monitor student progress or allow for questions
- Infrequently analyzes or lacks appropriate data
- Determines grades using only a few assignments
- Infrequently monitors or fails to monitor student progress
- Does not keep a communication log
- Does not record conferences with students or parents and guardians
- Uses extremes in grading—high failure rates or unrealistically high percentage of excellent grades
- Fails to reteach after assessments to correct gaps in student learning
- Uses only textbook assessments
- Records grades either incompletely or in an unclear way
- Does not include higher-order thinking questions or tasks in assessments
- Is slow in providing feedback
- Fails to acknowledge student achievement
- Offers little or no variety of assessments
- Ignores testing accommodations for students with special needs
- Does not document or holds few parent communications (communication may include conferences, phone calls, e-mail, newsletters, Web sites)
- Uses vague, technical, or inappropriate language in communications
- Does not participate in or attend IEP meetings for students with special needs

Professionalism

Teachers have been portrayed in a variety of ways in the media, ranging from detrimental influences to beloved masters of their craft who inspire students to excel. Effective teachers can be seen, heard, and sensed. The effective teacher engages in dialogue with students, colleagues, parents, and administrators and consistently demonstrates respect, accessibility, and expertise. Effective teachers are easily identified by their adept use of questioning and by the quality of instruction given in the classroom. Finally, an observer, who knows that this person truly makes a difference in the classroom, can sense the presence of an effective teacher. The true teacher is a master of teaching.

Positive Qualities

- Practices honest, two-way communication between teachers and administrators
- Communicates consistently with students' families
- Maintains accurate records
- Reflects on teaching, personally and with peers
- Is able to discuss teaching philosophy
- Attends grade-level meetings; is a true team player
- Attends and participates in faculty and other school committee meetings
- Focuses on students
- Performs assigned duties
- Implements school and school district goals and policies
- Acts "globally" around the school for the benefit of the whole school community
- Volunteers to assist others
- Seeks community involvement
- Seeks leadership roles on school committees and teams
- Contacts central office personnel for technical support when needed
- Treats colleagues with respect and collegiality
- Works collaboratively with faculty and staff
- Attends professional development opportunities (e.g., conferences, graduate classes, workshops)

- Maintains current teaching certification
- Initiates communication with parents
- Provides constructive feedback during meetings
- Supports school initiatives
- Mentors new teachers
- Submits required reports accurately and on time
- Writes constructive, grammatically correct communications
- Writes appropriately for the intended audience
- Evidences no testing irregularities that are within the control of the teacher
- Submits lesson plans and assessment documents on time
- Submits grades on time
- Maintains a calendar of report deadlines
- Keeps an accurate and complete grade book

Red Flags of Ineffective Teaching

- Routinely gives negative feedback at meetings
- Displays unwillingness to contribute to the mission and vision of the school
- Refuses to meet with parents and guardians or colleagues outside of contract hours
- Resents or feels threatened by other adults visiting the classroom
- Does the minimum required to maintain certification or emergency certification status
- Submits reports late or incomplete
- Submits grades late
- Writes inaccurate or unclear reports
- Does not update grade book or fails to keep it accurate
- Sends home notes that are illegible or contain grammatical and spelling errors
- Fails to return e-mail or phone calls
- Fails to respond to notes from parents
- Has problems with attendance
- Fails to maintain appropriate student and teacher roles

Positive Qualities and Red Flags for Teachers of At-Risk Students

Effective teachers of students at-risk display the same characteristics of effective teachers; however, teachers of students at-risk understand and accommodate for the unique challenges facing their students. They respond to students' academic, social, and emotional needs. The following list of positive qualities and red flags of ineffective teaching is not meant to be an exhaustive list, but one that underscores certain aspects of effective teaching.

Positive Qualities

- Gets to know students' cultures
- Inquires into issues facing the students' communities
- Believes that all students in difficult home environments can succeed
- Establishes rules and procedures on the first day of school
- Uses nonverbal cues to address inappropriate behavior
- Rewards positive behavior
- Ensures that students are exposed to content and skills that they are expected to know
- Engages students in higher-order thinking activities
- Uses a variety of instructional strategies
- Expects students to hand in completed work
- Uses both higher-level and lower-level questions in class
- Provides time for students to reflect on questions
- Makes specific written comments on assignments
- Provides specific feedback for correction without making general, negative comments such as "poor work"

Red Flags of Ineffective Teaching

- Believes that students cannot overcome familial and societal issues
- Refuses to offer help before or after school
- Lacks patience to deal with students' unique learning needs
- Emphasizes negative rather than positive reinforcement
- Doesn't make students aware of behavioral expectations
- Is described by students as "mean" or "unfair"
- Fails to intervene in difficult situations
- Fails to incorporate district or state subject standards into lesson plans

• Plans for mostly lower-level knowledge and comprehension of content and skills

• Uses the same few instructional strategies on a daily basis

• Accepts partially or poorly completed work without expectation of completion

• Uses mainly lower-level questions in classroom instruction

• Provides little to no wait time once a question has been asked

• Hands back assignments with little or no constructive feedback

• Makes general, negative comments about student work

Positive Qualities and Red Flags for Teachers of High-Ability Students

Teachers of high-ability students are effective at meeting the unique needs of their students. They exhibit the same characteristics of effective teachers, but display particular positive qualities when it comes to working with high-ability students. The red flags presented here stress the qualities that lead to ineffective teaching with this student population.

Positive Qualities

• Helps students pursue individual interests

• Is aware of the emotional needs of gifted students

• Views himself or herself as a lifelong learner

• Redirects aggressive learning behaviors

• Provides time for learning academic skills and social skills

• Finds ways to connect gifted students with experts in their field of interest

• Provides a multitude of resources in the classroom

• Uses pre-assessments to determine student knowledge prior to planning

• Provides time for student thought during questioning

• Incorporates technology into lessons

Red Flags of Ineffective Teaching

• Lacks training in gifted education

• Feels threatened by gifted students' knowledge base and aggressive learning

• Believes that gifted students will "get it anyway" and so do not need differentiation
• Lacks enthusiasm or knowledge of the subject taught
• Is disliked and not respected by students
• Organizes desks in the classroom in rows only
• Discourages student-to-student interaction
• Has every student working on the same activity or assignment on most days
• Mostly asks questions with "wrong" or "right" answers

Subject-Specific Qualities

Most teachers have been in an unfamiliar situation where they were not certain of what would be considered normal versus what would be considered questionable. For example, while a chemical fume hood would look out of place in a history classroom, it is a common element in a chemistry classroom. The following subject-specific qualities and red flags are shared to equip the reader with some indicators of what may be observed in effective and ineffective teachers' rooms in various disciplines.

English and Language Arts

An effective English teacher has a classroom that is text-rich and integrates the elements of the English language through writing, reading, and oral expression (including listening). The teacher is well read in the subject area and works diligently to convey enthusiasm for the subject. The teacher encourages reading great works of literature for class projects and for pleasure, maintains writing portfolios, provides opportunities for discussion, and gives plenty of feedback. In today's changing technological classrooms, software programs may be used to help enhance reading and writing instruction as well as research skills. The effective teacher's classroom integrates all key components of the English curriculum.

To enhance oral language in students, the teacher may do the following:
• Provide instruction in listening
• Model good listening behaviors
• Model reading aloud with appropriate voice and inflection
• Give instruction in speaking skills and verbal and nonverbal messages

• Provide activities for the preparation, practice, and presentation of formal speeches

• Demonstrate and practice the adaptation of oral communication strategies to match the needs of the situation and setting

• Offer opportunities to participate in role-plays, interviews, and impromptu speeches

• Lead discussion groups

• Give instruction in dialect, pronunciation, and articulation

• Use vocal elements in oral presentations: pitch, volume, rate, quality, animation, and pause

• Give instruction on how to use media for research, analysis, and evaluation of media messages

The teacher may use the following strategies in reading instruction:

• Read-alouds

• Independent reading

• Dyad reading (paired reading)

• Library visits to promote using the media center and facilitating appropriate book choice

• Classroom libraries with a variety of genres represented

• Blocks of time for student reading

• Student self-selection of reading materials

• Cause-and-effect frame

• Sequence of events

• Compare-and-contrast matrix

• Proposition and support outline

• Debriefing

• Discussion web

• Word wall and word bank

• Think-pair-share

• Literature circles

• Reader's workshop

Writing instruction may include these types of activities:

• POWER writing (prewriting, organizing, writing, editing, rewriting)

• Peer reviews and constructive criticism

• In-class writing and publishing center

• Writer's workshop
• District and national writing competitions
• Journals or learning logs
• Use of technology to facilitate the writing process
• Writing in different forms (technical, persuasive, research, expository, narrative, poetry)
    • Grammar instruction
    • Outlining
    • Note taking (e.g., Cornell notes)

History and Social Studies

The effective social studies teacher empowers students to think about history and the implications of past choices in order to guide thinking about the future or to find patterns within history. Students are taught a blend of essential facts and skills that enable them to access knowledge and make interpretations of history. The effective history or social studies teacher usually has an area of historical expertise that is evident in discussions and interactions with students on that period in history. Teachers use their understanding of how history works to teach students to construct their own personal bank of tools to critically examine current news and past events. The effective teacher finds ways to make the events of old become relevant to the students of today.

The teacher uses a variety of preteaching strategies including the following:

• K-W-L charts (know, want to know, learned)
• Learning logs
• Timelines
• Anticipation guides
• Graphic organizers

The teacher uses a variety of classroom practices:

• Simulations
• Debates
• Independent research projects
• Socratic seminars
• Historical inquiry
• Historical drama

• Internet- and technology-based activities
• Historical archives and analysis of primary documents, such as photographs, diaries, and government documents
• Three-dimensional (3-D) artifacts
• Current events
• Mapping (globes, wall maps, flat maps, computer maps, sketched maps)
• Mental mapping
• Literature-based lessons
• Critical thinking activities such as decision making, cause and effect, compare and contrast, and making inferences
• Visits to museums or virtual visits to museums if lacking in time and resources

The teacher may use a variety of assessment strategies:
• Cloze reading activities
• Multimedia presentations
• Reaction papers
• Historical interpretation
• Rubrics or scoring guides
• Performance-based assessments, such as interpreting a political cartoon
• Teacher-made tests, including multiple-choice, short-answer, and essay items

Mathematics

An effective mathematics teacher shows skill in facilitating students' ability to understand, analyze, and solve problems. The teacher presents real-world applications of math concepts to make the application pertinent to students. The teacher helps students to think beyond the paper and the pencil to comprehend how mathematics is evident and applied to everyday life. The room is probably filled with manipulatives and decorated with math-related posters and 3-D constructions. The chalkboard tray holds oversized replicas of the tools students use, such as protractors and compasses. The teacher uses these tools to break down the process and provide meaning for the class. If a student is having difficulty, the teacher is able to diagnose and remediate the gap in prior knowledge or identify where the student has misunderstood the process to get the child back on track. Students are asked to compute problems, write about solutions, and discuss mathematics. Mathematics is not just numbers and symbols; it is a language for understanding.

The mathematics teacher uses a variety of tools and manipulatives to teach, including the following:
- Various papers (grid, dot, patty, graphing, notebook)
- Calculators (four-function, scientific, graphing)
- Measurement tools (angle ruler, balance, compass, protractor, ruler, thermometer)
- Mathematical software programs and spreadsheets
- Commercial manipulatives (algebra tiles, cubes, Cuisenaire rods, decimal blocks, fraction circles, geoboards, Hands-on Algebra, tangrams)
- Common materials (spinners, coins, dice, yarn)
- Chalkboards or white boards that have grids
- Overhead calculator and transparent tiles

The effective mathematics teacher uses a variety of approaches to teaching the content, including the following:
- Application problems using real-life data
- 3-D constructions
- Reading and writing story problems
- Using visuals in problems
- Mental mathematics
- Prediction and estimation
- Discussing mathematical concepts
- Students talking through how to do the problem
- Tessellations
- Examining musical patterns in algebra
- Considering angles and proportions in art when studying measurement
- Venn diagrams

Science

Scientific discoveries are constantly adding to and changing the body of science knowledge. Effective teachers engage students in experimentation and discussion of the findings. They are aware of changes and highlight new and older discoveries with students as, together, they investigate and develop an understanding of science.

The science classroom has safety as a focus, with the following items displayed or easily available:

- Posted safety rules
- Lab safety contracts
- Available protective materials (lab aprons, gloves, goggles)
- Fire extinguisher or fire blanket in rooms using flammable materials
- Classroom shut-off valves that are labeled, if present
- Chemicals are stored with materials safety data sheets
- Marked disposal bin for broken glass
- Eyewash
- Locked chemical storage

The science teacher uses a variety of techniques to facilitate the learning of the curriculum objectives:

- Cooperative learning groups
- Inquiry-based instruction and learning
- Computer simulations
- Laboratory investigations and experiments
- Lab write-ups
- Scientific models
- Project-based learning
- Hands-on activities
- Demonstrations
- Reading scientific articles and journals
- Graphic organizers

The science classroom contains a variety of equipment, including the following:

- Beakers, flasks, and graduated cylinders
- Rulers, compasses, and protractors
- Scales and balances
- Computer-based laboratory probes
- Graphing calculators and scientific calculators
- Plant grow light
- Dissection tools
- Microscopes

- Models
- Thermometers
- Chemicals
- Lenses, prisms, and mirrors

Summary

A teacher cannot simply be deemed effective because he or she possesses the qualities itemized in this section. Likewise, red flags do not necessarily signal an ineffective teacher, just a behavior that needs improvement. Just as teachers must differentiate for student needs, additional qualities and red flags may be applicable to your unique situation. Teachers are effective because of how various personal and professional factors combine and are executed in a classroom.

Section III

Annotated Bibliography

Reference	Prerequisites	The Person	Management and Organization	Planning for Instruction	Implementing Instruction	Monitoring Progress and Potential	Teachers of At-Risk Students	Teachers of High-Ability Students
Cawelti, 1999		•		•	•	•		
Cawelti, 2004				•	•	•		
Corbett & Wilson, 2002		•	•		•		•	
Cotton, 2000		•	•	•	•	•		
Cunningham & Allington, 1999				•	•			
Darling-Hammond, 2000	•	•		•	•	•		
Darling-Hammond, Berry, & Thoreson, 2001	•							
Darling-Hammond, Holtzman, Gatlin, & Heilig, 2005	•						•	
Emmer, Evertson, & Anderson, 1980		•	•	•	•			
Ferguson & Womack, 1993	•							
Fetler, 1999	•							
Goldhaber & Brewer, 2000	•							
Good & Brophy, 1997		•	•	•	•			
Hansen & Feldhusen, 1994	•			•	•			•
Hanushek, 1971	•		•					
Hawk, Coble, & Swanson, 1985	•							

Reference	Prerequisites	The Person	Management and Organization	Planning for Instruction	Implementing Instruction	Monitoring Progress and Potential	Teachers of At-Risk Students	Teachers of High-Ability Students
Haycock, 2000	•						•	
Johnson, 1997	•	•	•	•	•	•		
Karnes & Bean, 2001			•	•	•	•		•
Marzano, 2003			•	•	•	•		
Marzano (with Marzano & Pickering), 2003		•	•					
Marzano, Pickering, & McTighe, 1993		•	•	•	•	•		
Mason, Schroeter, Combs, & Washington, 1992	•		•	•	•	•		
McBer, 2000		•						
Miller, McKenna, & McKenna, 1998	•				•			
Monk & King,1994	•	•						
National Association of Secondary School Principals, 1997	•	•			•			
Peart & Campbell, 1999	•	•	•	•	•	•	•	
Pressley, Raphael, Gallagher, & DiBella, 2004		•			•	•	•	
Rowan, Chiang, & Miller, 1997	•	•						
Shellard & Protheroe, 2000					•			
VanTassel-Baska & Little, 2003	•		•	•	•	•		•
Walsh & Sattes, 2005					•			
Wang, Haertel, & Walberg, 1993b			•	•	•	•		
Weiss & Pasley, 2004					•		•	
Wenglinsky, 2004					•	•	•	
Westberg & Archambault, 1997	•			•	•			•
Willard-Holt, 2003					•	•		•
Williams, 2003	•	•			•	•	•	

Cawelti, G. (1999). *Portraits of Six Benchmark Schools: Diverse Approaches to Improving Student Achievement.* Arlington, VA: Educational Research Service. [Monograph].

Keywords: The Person, Planning for Instruction, Implementing Instruction, Monitoring Progress and Potential

Summary: Six schools from around the country are profiled as models for their approaches to meeting the needs of challenging students. Although the schools have different approaches to creating high standards for student achievement, they have specific factors in common. The common factors include a focus on standards, teamwork, the principal as an instructional leader, changes to the student's instructional life, and dedicated teachers. In all six schools, the teachers' foundational commitment to student success is instrumental in the quality of the approaches taken by schools. On a daily basis, the teachers implement strategies to promote student success. Common denominators of these benchmark schools include teachers committed to the daily task of preparing students, high standards, an environment designed to ensure success, and unpredicted achievement at high levels based on student characteristics. In addition, the model schools link their programs to state-established standards and develop high-quality staff development practices. Parental support is strong and includes the monitoring of assignments by parents. For students who require additional assistance, summer programs are available.

Each of the six profiled schools is unique in its approach to meeting the needs of the student population. Strong leadership is vital in giving direction, and the teachers are exemplary in their dedication to being accountable in order to effect change.

Cawelti, G. (Ed.). (2004). *Handbook of Research on Improving Student Achievement* (3rd ed.). Arlington, VA: Educational Research Service. [Handbook].

Keywords: Planning for Instruction, Implementing Instruction, Monitoring Progress and Potential

Summary: This research-based compendium of classroom practices for enhancing student achievement was compiled for use by teachers, principals, other instructional leaders, and policymakers. In addition to providing information on specific educational practices, the book contains feedback from users of the first edition of *Handbook of Research on Improving Student Achievement.* The handbook discusses the productive use of this information in six broad categories:

1. *Teacher and staff development.* The handbook is a useful tool for validating the instructional practices that teachers are already employing.

2. *Curriculum development and improvement.* School districts use the handbook to strengthen weaknesses that are identified by standardized tests.

3. *Teacher evaluation process.* The handbook can be used as a resource by principals when observing teachers.

4. *Development activities and a reference for principals and other administrators.* Information from the handbook is useful for administrators in preparing presentations for association meetings.

5. *School improvement and planning activities.* Districts will find the handbook useful in systematic curriculum review.

6. *Higher education programs.* College and university professors will be able to use the handbook as a graduate-level textbook.

The handbook is also a resource for the specific disciplines in K–12 classrooms. It addresses practices for use in the arts, foreign language, health education, language arts, mathematics, oral communications, physical education, science, and social studies.

Corbett, D., & Wilson, B. (2002). What Urban Students Say About Good Teaching. *Educational Leadership, 60*(1), 18–22. [Journal].

Keywords: The Person, Management and Organization, Implementing Instruction, Teachers of At-Risk Students

Summary: Researchers interviewed approximately 400 urban, low-income middle school students over a three-year period in order to examine the students' experiences in school and their views of good teaching. The schools that these students attended were undergoing districtwide reform. The researchers' findings detail student perceptions of good teaching.

The students first and foremost attributed the success of their learning to their teachers. Furthermore, they consistently identified six qualities of effective teaching:

1. Pushing students on a daily basis to be successful and to put forth their best effort.

2. Managing the classroom by maintaining control over behavior and classroom procedures.

3. Being able to determine the type of help students need and providing that help to students.

4. Finding ways to explain the content until all students have a firm grasp of it.

5. Using a variety of instructional activities.

6. Working to understand students as persons, not just as students in the classroom.

The researchers found that students do care about their own learning and they view an effective teacher as a central element to their success.

Cotton, K. (2000). *The Schooling Practices That Matter Most.* **Portland, OR: Northwest Regional Educational Laboratory; and Alexandria, VA: Association for Supervision and Curriculum Development. [Booklet].**

Keywords: The Person, Management and Organization, Planning for Instruction, Implementing Instruction, Monitoring Progress and Potential

Summary: In this booklet written for classroom teachers, the author outlines the contextual and instructional factors drawn from the long list of known effective educational practices that she feels "enable virtually all students to learn successfully." The author states that she omitted factors such as school size and socioeconomic status because educators can only minimally affect them. The scope of this booklet is limited to those factors that can be addressed by teachers.

Cotton identifies 10 contextual factors: academically heterogeneous class assignments; flexible in-class grouping; maximized learning time; monitoring of student progress; parent and community involvement; primary focus on learning; a safe and orderly school environment; small class size; strong administrative leadership; and a supportive classroom climate. He also identifies five instructional attributes: careful orientation to lessons; clear and focused instruction; effective questioning techniques; feedback and reinforcement; and review and researching as needed.

In addition, Cotton explains that not all of these "critical attributes" need to be present for a student to learn well. The families of some students may provide enough experiences and support to effectively compensate for an attribute lacking in a particular school. Individual students may have enough innate ability that they learn well in less-than-ideal conditions. The author maintains that all of these attributes need to be present for all students to learn.

Cunningham, P. M., & Allington, R. L. (1999). *Classrooms That Work: They Can All Read and Write.* **New York: Longman. [Book].**

Keywords: Planning for Instruction, Implementing Instruction

Summary: In this examination of successful reading and writing strategies for primary and intermediate school students, the authors note that educators historically have faced various obstacles in their efforts to develop literacy in their students. The authors describe these problems and present specific approaches to help students overcome their illiteracy challenges. Of primary importance is the need for authentic writing and reading activities to be central to the curriculum and the school day if students are to become literate. Specific strategies are successful in guiding and supporting reading and writing for all students and for those who have particular difficulty with learning to read. The book presents activities that increase students' decoding and spelling fluency by teaching them to pronounce, spell, and look for patterns in words. Both the development of knowledge specific to science and social studies and the promotion of reading, writing, and vocabulary in learning these disciplines are examined. The authors present techniques that enable educators to integrate the components critical to learning in kindergarten, primary, and intermediate classrooms throughout the day and week. In addition, larger school and social issues, such as class size and community involvement, have an impact on literacy.

Darling-Hammond, L. (2000). Teacher Quality and Student Achievement: A Review of State Policy Evidence. *Educational Policy Analysis Archives, 8*(1). **[Online journal article]. Available: http://epaa.asu/ epaa.asu.edu/epaa/v8n1/**

Keywords: Prerequisites, The Person, Planning for Instruction, Implementing Instruction, Monitoring Progress and Potential

Summary: This 50-state study of policies on teacher education, licensing, hiring, and professional development indicates a relationship between teacher quality and student achievement. The data are based on results from the 1993–94 Schools and Staffing Surveys and the National Assessment of Educational Progress (NAEP), along with case studies and policy surveys. The results show a correlation of teacher preparation and certification to student reading and mathematics achievement before and after controlling for language and poverty. Criteria for teacher preparation range from requirements for a bachelor's degree in states with high student achievement to requirements for only six weeks of student teaching in other states. Since the 1980s, when the United States began investing in teacher preparation in reading, students' achievement has compared favorably with that of students in other countries. In the Third International Mathematics and Science Study (TIMSS) of 25 nations, U.S. students ranked 18th in mathematics and 17th in physics, with 50 percent of the country's physics teachers uncertified or having no minor in the field.

The results of Darling-Hammond's study indicate that teachers certified or degreed in their teaching field correlate positively with higher student outcomes in reading and mathematics. Students in poverty and of non-English-speaking status are more likely to have uncertified teachers. Class size and pupil-teacher ratios do not seem to correlate to student achievement. The teacher's verbal ability, content knowledge, licensing exam scores, and professional development do seem to affect student achievement positively.

Darling-Hammond, L., Berry, B., & Thoreson, A. (2001). Does Teacher Certification Matter? Evaluating the Evidence. *Educational Evaluation and Policy Analysis*, **23**(1), 57–77. [Journal article].

Keywords: Prerequisites

Summary: The authors present alternate conclusions to those reached by Goldhaber and Brewer (2000), who propose from their research that states eliminate teacher certification requirements. According to Darling-Hammond and colleagues, the data upon which Goldhaber and Brewer's proposal were based included 24 math and 34 science teachers, a minute percentage of the total sample of 3,469 teachers. From Goldhaber and Brewer's data, Darling-Hammond and coauthors conclude that certified teachers have a greater influence on student achievement than teachers with only a degree in their teaching field. This suggests that the preparation necessitated by state certification requirements is likely to increase subject-matter competence. In addition, emergency and temporary certification status is nonrenewable by most standards after one to two years. In most states, teachers who hold these types of credentials are fully qualified educators who can be classified in one of the following categories: certified in another state; returning after a hiatus from teaching; or fully qualified in another field or in their teaching field except for completion of one course or test.

The authors reinterpret the data as follows. Students of experienced, certified teachers had significantly higher achievement than students of less-experienced teachers with nonstandard certification. An education degree is a major factor contributing to higher achievement, along with years of teaching experience. Degrees in the field and in education have a positive influence on student achievement. Students of experienced teachers with standard certification have significantly higher achievement in math and science than students of less-experienced teachers with nonstandard certification. Critical to the issue of certification is the vast variability in standard and alternative teacher preparation programs.

Darling-Hammond, L., Holtzman, D. J., Gatlin, S. J., & Heilig, J. V. (2005). Does Teacher Preparation Matter? Evidence About Teacher Certification, Teach for America, and Teacher Effectiveness. *Education Policy Analysis Archives, 13*(42). [Online journal article]. Available: http://epaa.asu.edu/epaa/v13n42/

Keywords: Prerequisites, Teachers of At-Risk Students

This study examined a large student-level data set from Houston, Texas. Researchers worked to link detailed certification data on teachers to background and achievement data on students, classrooms, and schools for 132,071 4th and 5th grade students, which led to data on 4,408 teachers. The data set allowed examinations of whether Teach for America (TFA) candidates (recruits from selective universities who receive a few weeks of training before they begin teaching) were as effective as similarly experienced certified teachers. The findings indicated the following:

• Certified teachers consistently produced significantly stronger student achievement gains than did uncertified teachers.

• Uncertified TFA recruits were less effective than certified teachers, and performed about as well as other uncertified teachers.

• TFA recruits who became certified after two or three years did about as well as other certified teachers in supporting student achievement gains. However, TFA teachers left their teaching positions in Houston by their third year at rates between 57 percent to 90 percent.

• Teachers lacking full certification slowed student progress up to a month on grade-equivalent tests. If generalized, students from the most affected schools who have uncertified teachers each year could fall one to two years behind grade level by 6th grade.

In summary, the researchers found that teachers' effectiveness appeared strongly related to the preparation they received for teaching.

Emmer, E. T., Evertson, C. M., & Anderson, L. M. (1980). Effective Classroom Management at the Beginning of the School Year. *The Elementary School Journal, 80*(5), 219–231. [Journal article].

Keywords: The Person, Management and Organization, Organizing for Instruction, Implementing Instruction

Summary: This study examines how effective and less-effective teachers differ in behavior management, instruction, student concerns, and constraints. The study considers personality characteristics of 27 3rd grade teachers who were observed throughout the year with a focus on their initial strategies to start the year. Based on the observations, teacher interviews, and factors that established comparable classrooms, the teachers were divided into two groups, for which the only difference was effectiveness. Seven teachers were included in the effective managers group, and seven teachers were included in the less-effective group.

Less-effective teachers tended to issue general criticisms such as "some children are too noisy" rather than addressing specific students. They had difficulty employing individualized instruction while other students engaged in off-task behavior. Instructions for seatwork were vague, and no monitoring was done to evaluate student understanding of expectations. They did not anticipate or plan for problems and were distracted from the class when problems impeded classroom operations.

The study concluded that more effective teachers spend maximum contact time with students the first day. They reinforce rules by explaining them to students and reminding them; are good monitors of behavior and promptly stop inappropriate behavior; and anticipate and work out procedures to address student needs. Effective teachers give clear, detailed instructions; anticipate student attention spans when designing lessons; and anticipate and compensate for constraints such as a lack of supplies. These teachers have higher levels of student engagement and lower levels of off-task behaviors, as well as higher ratings for listening and expressing feelings. Both groups of teachers in the study treated students equitably.

Ferguson, P., & Womack, S. T. (1993). The Impact of Subject Matter and Education Coursework on Teaching Performance. *Journal of Teacher Education, 44*(1), 55–63. [Journal article].

Keywords: Prerequisites

Summary: This three-year study focuses on the graduates of Arkansas Tech University's teacher education program to evaluate the effectiveness of the university's program and to see to what extent coursework can be used to predict performance of the student teachers. Cooperating teachers, content specialists, student teaching supervisors, school of education student teaching supervisors, and the student teachers' evaluations on a 107-item Likert-response survey were used. Data from the four sources were collected for 266 students.

The results of the study indicated that coursework is the strongest predictor of teaching performance. Grade point average (GPA) and National Teacher Exam specialty scores account for less than 4 percent of the variance in teacher performance. Increased coursework in the content area at the expense of pedagogical coursework will be counterproductive. Raising the GPA requirements above 2.5 for acceptance into teacher education programs will unnecessarily reject 63 percent of the participants in the study. Teacher education makes a difference in teaching performance.

The studies cited in the literature review reinforce the researchers' findings that subject-matter preparation is important, but not sufficient by itself. The impact of teacher education is documented, showing a positive relationship between teacher education coursework and student achievement. In addition, the literature review indicates that not only did alternatively prepared teachers have more difficulty in day-to-day teaching than traditionally prepared teachers, but also that certified teachers are more effective than teachers with less formal training.

Fetler, M. (1999). High School Staff Characteristics and Mathematics Test Results. *Educational Policy Analysis Archives,* **7(9). [Online journal article]. Available: http://epaa.asu.edu/epaa/v7n9.html**

Keywords: Prerequisites

Summary: In this California study, mathematics teachers with majors and minors in the subject were found to have students with higher test scores. The study was conducted to determine if the shortage in qualified math teachers results in lower test scores in high school mathematics. The Stanford Achievement Test (Stanford 9) and the annual state survey Professional Assignment Information Form results were used to determine how teachers' educational level and years of service affect student achievement. The issues of teacher preparation and experience were addressed after factoring out the impact of poverty. In this study of mathematics teachers, 10.5 percent had emergency permits, and 60 percent had been teaching for 10 or more years.

Student test scores increased from grades 9 to 11 as a factor of student attrition and selective testing, as high-performing students elected to take upper-level mathematics courses. Schools with higher levels of poverty tended to have fewer well-prepared teachers and lower test scores. Teacher experience and preparation were significantly related to achievement when poverty was factored out. The more experienced and educated the staff, the higher the student achievement test scores will be. Schools with higher percentages of teachers on emergency permits tended to have lower test scores. The researcher suggests that the shortage of qualified mathematics teachers lowers student achievement scores.

The author also suggests strategies for recruiting qualified teachers, including staff development for unqualified teachers, increasing undergraduate requirements for college mathematics, and establishing a uniform assessment of the subject-matter knowledge required to teach high school math successfully.

Goldhaber, D. D., & Brewer, D. J. (2000). Does Teacher Certification Matter? High School Teacher Certification Status and Student Achievement. *Educational Evaluation and Policy Analysis,* 22(2), 129–145. [Journal article].

Keywords: Prerequisites

Summary: This study examines the impact of teacher certification and state-by-state differences in teacher licensure requirements on student performance. The researchers tested whether students of teachers possessing emergency, probationary, or private school certification have lower scores than students of teachers with standard certification. Of the teachers, 86 percent had standard certification in math, and 82 percent had standard certification in science. In a follow-up survey of high school seniors, from the National Educational Longitudinal Study of 1988, the following results were found:

• Students with teachers with standard or private school certification in mathematics show a 7- to 10-point gain in math test scores in 10th and 12th grades.

• Students who perform poorly in math in a previous grade are more likely to be assigned in 12th grade to a teacher without standard certification.

• Teachers with higher scores on a state certification exam have students with higher scores on math examinations.

• Math teachers with increased college coursework in mathematics have higher-performing students.

No mention is made in the study as to the high school math levels that these teachers teach. No evidence is found that supports the belief that standard certified teachers outperform those teachers with emergency certifications. The authors speculate that school divisions may have more carefully screened these emergency certified teachers for ability and content knowledge. However, students whose teachers are teaching outside their field in math perform more poorly than students whose teachers have standard certifications in math.

Good, T. L., & Brophy, J. E. (1997). **Increasing Teacher Awareness Through Observation. In T. L. Good & J. E. Brophy,** *Looking in Classrooms* **(7th ed.). New York: Addison-Wesley. [Textbook].**

Keywords: The Person, Management and Organization, Planning for Instruction, Implementing Instruction

Summary: Teachers receive a great deal of information throughout the course of the day and must make spontaneous decisions. Often teachers are unaware of classroom events because the interactions are rapid, they are sensitive to different stimuli, they are not taught to monitor and study their instructional behavior, and feedback to teachers about their own classroom behavior is rare. The reality is that teachers are very busy preparing lessons, interacting with students, and providing feedback. This chapter considers the benefits of increasing teachers' awareness of classroom interactions and indicates areas for improvement. The authors suggest that teachers take the following actions:

• Interpret and respond to student behavior immediately.

• Focus on giving meaning to instruction, model techniques for acquiring information from reading, and provide opportunities to apply the skill.

• Call on all students, not just the most capable; give frequent praise.

• Balance attention given to each gender during particular subjects.

• Allocate time based on what is being accomplished instructionally and maximize interactive instructional time.

• Vary assignments and opportunities for the learner.

• Give all students, regardless of ability, equal amounts of time to respond to questions.

To increase effectiveness, teachers may benefit from observing their own teaching through the use of technology or from reflections of observers. The authors suggest that in reviewing videotapes, trained consultants are a valuable resource to help the teacher identify what to look for in the lesson.

Hansen, J., & Feldhusen, J. F. (1994). **Comparison of Trained and Untrained Teachers of Gifted Students.** *Gifted Child Quarterly,* **38(3), 115–123. [Journal article].**

Keywords: Prerequisites, Planning for Instruction, Implementing Instruction, Teachers of High-Ability Students

Summary: Gifted and talented students typically have a higher-than-average IQ and special abilities that often qualify them for accelerated classes or additional resources to address their unique needs. Teachers trained to meet the unique learning needs of these students often have coursework in the nature of giftedness, characteristics of gifted learners, and advanced instructional strategies to serve students either in special programs or in the general classroom. The teaching practices of 54 trained teachers (three to five graduate courses in gifted education) were compared to 28 untrained teachers (no graduate coursework in gifted education) using trained observers and questionnaires administered to both students and teachers. Researchers found major differences between untrained teachers and trained teachers in their teaching abilities and classroom climates. Trained teachers of gifted students created more positive classroom environments and used more effective teaching practices than did their untrained colleagues. Students of trained teachers rated their teachers significantly higher than did students of untrained teachers. Trained teachers scored significantly higher on 11 dimensions: subject-matter coverage, clarity of teaching, motivational techniques, pace of instruction, student-directed activities, variety of student experiences, student-teacher interaction, higher-level thinking, creativity, teacher planning, and instructional aides. Trained teachers used lecture significantly less than untrained teachers, and they focused more on conceptualization than on the study of isolated facts. The authors conclude that training in gifted education does make a difference in a teacher's ability to meet the needs of gifted students.

Hanushek, E. (1971). Teacher Characteristics and Gains in Student Achievement: Estimation Using Micro Data. *American Economic Review, 61*(2), 280–288. [Journal article].

Keywords: Prerequisites, Management and Organization

Summary: Various factors, including characteristics of K–3 teachers, were evaluated for their effect on student achievement in a California school with large Mexican American and Caucasian populations. The teacher characteristics included level of education, teaching experience, and verbal facility, which was defined as intelligence and communication skills. Data used in the study included student Stanford Achievement Test scores, teacher surveys, and scores from a verbal facility test given to teachers.

The analysis indicates that the teacher makes a significant difference in the performance of white students, but does not affect the achievement of Mexican American students, who progressed at a slower rate regardless of the teacher.

It was also shown that 3rd graders with a teacher with recent educational experiences showed 0.2 to 0.3 years of additional gain in reading achievement. Verbal ability significantly affects achievement for a specific population of white children, but does not affect the achievement of other students. Teaching experience and graduate degrees do not contribute to gains in student achievement scores except for a specific white population. Language may be a barrier for the Mexican American students in this school district. More time spent on discipline negatively affects achievement.

Hawk, P. P., Coble, C. R., & Swanson, M. (1985). Certification: It Does Matter. *Journal of Teacher Education, 36*(3), 13–15. [Journal article].

Keywords: Prerequisites

Summary: This study investigated the differences between certified and uncertified mathematics teachers in middle and high school in the areas of student achievement, content knowledge, and instructional presentation skills. Noncertified teachers were characterized as those who were not certified in the area of mathematics but did possess state certification in another field. The study matched 18 certified and 18 noncertified teachers in the same school teaching the same mathematics course to 826 students of similar ability; however, the teachers were not matched by years of experience. The pretest scores of these students on the Stanford Achievement Test for general math and the Stanford Test of Academic Skills for algebra did not differ significantly. To consider professional skills, trained observers conducted classroom observations. The teachers took the Descriptive Tests of Mathematics Skills to measure their mathematical knowledge. Five months later, the students were given the same Stanford test as a post-test to assess student achievement.

The study found that student achievement was greater for students taught by teachers certified in their field. Certified teachers scored significantly higher on instructional presentation, suggesting that those who are more knowledgeable in their field are more successful in presenting material to students. In algebra, certified teachers scored significantly higher on content knowledge. Teacher demographics such as years of teaching experience or type of degree earned did not significantly affect student achievement or teacher performance. The results suggest that the factors of content knowledge and instructional strategies for teachers teaching in their field combine to increase student achievement.

Haycock, K. (2000). No More Settling for Less. *Thinking K–16, 4*(1), 3–12. [Journal article].

Keywords: Prerequisites, Teachers of At-Risk Students

Summary: Certification, strong content background, classroom experience, and cumulative effects of teacher quality were considered in a study of the distribution of qualified teachers in the schools of children of color and lower socioeconomic status. The results indicate a disparity in the number of qualified teachers among ethnic groups and socioeconomic status. High school students in high-poverty (greater than 75 percent) and/or high-minority (greater than 90 percent) schools are twice as likely to have noncertified teachers as students in low-poverty (less than 10 percent) and/or low-minority (less than 10 percent) schools. Approximately 23 percent of teachers lack certification in their subject areas. Teachers of mathematics are more likely not to be certified in their teaching field than any other core content area teacher. Students with teachers scoring higher on mathematics and verbal skill tests achieve at higher levels than students with lower-scoring teachers. Schools with high concentrations of minority and poor students were more likely to have inexperienced, unlicensed, or alternatively licensed teachers.

Reducing class size tended to increase the possibility of placing an uncertified reading teacher in a California classroom from 1 percent to 12 percent. Differences within schools were found in honors and advanced placement classes. Teachers of these classes were more likely to be certified and to have more years of teaching experience. The classes tended to have disproportionate numbers of Asian, white, and upper-income students.

Suggestions to alleviate the situation included raising standards for teacher licensure, professional development, and university teacher preparation programs in order to ensure qualified teachers in all classrooms.

Johnson, B. L. (1997). An Organizational Analysis of Multiple Perspectives of Effective Teaching: Implications for Teacher Evaluation. *Journal of Personnel Evaluation in Education, 11,* 69–87. [Journal article].

Keywords: Prerequisites, The Person, Management and Organization, Planning for Instruction, Implementing Instruction, Monitoring Progress and Potential

Summary: Urban, suburban, and rural school board members, principals, and teachers from elementary, middle, and secondary schools were interviewed to determine their concepts of effective teaching and to reflect on the effect of the educator's role on teacher evaluation policy. Their descriptions of effective teaching were categorized as teacher as person, teaching process, and teaching product.

Teachers provided the most descriptors of effective teaching, followed by principals and school board members. Board members emphasized product, while the principals and teachers focused on process and person, using descriptors such as instructional strategies, identification of lesson objectives, monitoring and assessing students, student-centeredness, positive learning environment, and flexibility of instruction. All three groups recognized the importance of the following attributes:

- Teacher as person—knowledge and caring.
- Teaching process—classroom control and communication.
- Teaching product—on-task behavior and process/learning/mastery.

Only teachers included teacher outcomes in their descriptors. The greatest level of consensus within a group was among teachers, which may have been attributable to the common experience of the teacher training programs that many completed.

Descriptors that maximize the commonalities and are specific enough to warrant teacher acceptance may have implications for construction of a teacher evaluation model. As a result of the study, the author defined effective teaching this way: "Effective teaching involves a two-way communicative process initiated by a teacher who is well versed in the subject matter, caring, and able to establish and maintain classroom control. In such a setting students are continually attentive and progress in their learning."

Karnes, F. A., & Bean, S. M. (Eds.). (2001). *Methods and Materials for Teaching the Gifted and Talented.* **Waco, TX: Prufrock Press. [Book].**

Keywords: Management and Organization, Planning for Instruction, Implementing Instruction, Monitoring Progress and Potential, Teachers of High-Ability Students

Summary: Students with exceptional abilities, as with any other students, have unique needs and are as varied and diverse as the general student population. The editors of this book have compiled the thinking of best practices in managing the classroom, planning for instruction, implementing instruction, and assessing student learning. The book is divided into four sections:

• Characteristics and Needs of Gifted Learners—The two chapters in this section focus on the social, emotional, and academic needs of students with high abilities and ways to manage the classroom environment to enhance student learning.

• Instructional Planning and Evaluation—Six chapters detail curriculum planning for high-ability students both at the district and individual school level, as well as assessment of student learning.

• Strategies for Best Practice—The heart of the book focuses on instructional strategies for gifted students. In these 10 chapters, the authors provide detailed descriptions of best practices along with strategies for implementation.

• Supporting and Enhancing Gifted Programs—The final three chapters examine the challenge of obtaining resources for use in the gifted classroom and the role of the teacher and of those involved in planning gifted programs in advocating for the needs of the gifted.

The book provides a comprehensive examination of the needs of high-ability students along with specific instructional strategies to meet those needs.

Marzano, R. J. (2003). *What Works in Schools.* **Alexandria, VA: Association for Supervision and Curriculum Development. [Book].**

Keywords: Management and Organization, Planning for Instruction, Implementing Instruction, Monitoring Progress and Potential

Summary: This book details the school-level, teacher-level, and student-level factors that affect student achievement. A synthesis of teacher-level research reveals the following conclusions:

• Some teachers are more effective than others, as determined by student achievement gains.

• Most-effective and least-effective teachers can have cumulative effects on student learning.

• The effectiveness of the school and of the teacher has an impact on the academic achievement of the average student.

The author reviewed relevant research and developed three factors that have an impact on a teacher's effectiveness: instructional strategies, classroom management, and classroom curriculum design. An implementation model for school reform is offered to address factors that not only relate to teacher effectiveness but also school effectiveness, as well as the student-level factors that affect achievement. The model is based on three principles:

• Principle 1: Reform is highly contextual.
• Principle 2: Reform must be based on data.
• Principle 3: Change must be incremental.

These principles form the underlying basis for addressing teacher-level factors, school-level factors, and student-level factors that affect student learning.

Marzano, R. J., with Marzano, J. S., & Pickering, D. J. (2003). *Classroom Management That Works.* **Alexandria, VA: Association for Supervision and Curriculum Development. [Book].**

Keywords: The Person, Management and Organization

Summary: The ability to manage a classroom is offered as a critical quality of an effective teacher. The author synthesized relevant research on four specific aspects of classroom management. Each of the four aspects was found to be significant in successful management of the classroom. The critical aspects, along with their effect sizes, are listed below:

- The importance of rules and procedures (ES −.763).
- The effects of disciplinary interventions (ES −.909).
- The crucial relationship between teachers and students (ES −.869).
- The development of a frame of mind to deal with classroom management issues (ES −1.294).

Each of these four elements was significant in successful management of the classroom. In discussions of each factor, relevant research and theory are explored and detailed, programs to address each factor are discussed, and action steps to improve on each of the factors are offered.

Marzano, R. J., Pickering, D., & McTighe, J. (1993). *Assessing Student Outcomes: Performance Assessment Using the Dimensions of Learning Model*. Alexandria, VA: Association for Supervision and Curriculum Development. [Book].

Keywords: The Person, Management and Organization, Planning for Instruction, Implementing Instruction, Monitoring Progress and Potential

Summary: Dimensions of Learning, an instructional framework based on learning theory and research, is designed to help teachers become more effective in planning curriculum and instruction and in teaching to performance assessment. The theory focuses on five dimensions of learning or types of thinking that are vital for learning to occur.

- *Dimension 1: Positive Attitudes and Perceptions About Learning.* Learning increases when students feel comfortable in a classroom environment perceived as safe and orderly.
- *Dimension 2: Acquiring and Integrating Knowledge.* Instructional strategies should enable students to relate new knowledge to prior knowledge. As connections are made, information will be stored in long-term memory.
- *Dimension 3: Extending and Refining Knowledge.* Appropriate activities that extend and refine knowledge will enable the teacher to integrate the teaching of content and cognitive skills.
- *Dimension 4: Using Knowledge Meaningfully.* Instruction that enables students to apply information in meaningful ways significantly enhances

learning. The five types of tasks that contribute to meaningful application of knowledge are decision making, investigation, experimental inquiry, problem solving, and invention.

• *Dimension 5: Productive Habits of Mind.* Developing students' minds to be self-disciplined and to think critically and creatively will enable students to become self-motivated, lifelong learners.

The five dimensions are intertwined and cannot be implemented piecemeal. Incorporation of these types of thinking in development and delivery of curriculum will strengthen the link between instruction and learning and assessment.

Mason, D. A., Schroeter, D. D., Combs, R. K., & Washington, K. (1992). Assigning Average-Achieving Eighth Graders to Advanced Mathematics Classes in an Urban Junior High. *The Elementary School Journal, 92*(5), 587–599. [Journal article].

Keywords: Prerequisites, Management and Organization, Planning for Instruction, Implementing Instruction, Monitoring Progress and Potential

Summary: Average-achieving 8th grade students were placed in a pre-algebra class for high-achieving students. Traditionally they would have been placed in general mathematics classes. Thirty-four average-ability students took the pre-algebra course with a highly effective teacher who had a master's degree in mathematics and regularly took advanced coursework and workshops to enhance teaching skills. The study attributed the high achievement of these students to the following:

• The teacher.

• Use of expectation theory and communication of teacher confidence in student ability to succeed with appropriate effort.

• Workshops on active teaching.

• Use of techniques identified by the National Council of Teachers of Mathematics (NCTM), such as an integrative approach to problem solving.

• Application of word problems to the students' experiences.

• Cooperative learning techniques.

• Opportunities for tutoring from the teacher on an as-needed basis.

The program saw a gradual increase in student scores on the Comprehensive Assessment Program Achievement Series Test during the three years of implementation. High-achieving students scored significantly higher than average-achieving students; however, several students in the average-achieving group scored higher than the high-achieving students. The higher-achieving students earned higher grades in the class. Follow-up examinations of the students' high school records showed that average-achieving students who took pre-algebra as 8th graders enrolled more often in advanced math classes than their general math cohorts. The on-grade-level students, who returned to the general mathematics curriculum in 9th grade, earned higher grades than their cohorts in the general math program.

McBer, H. (2000). *Research into Teacher Effectiveness: A Model of Teacher Effectiveness.* (Research Report #216). Nottingham, England: Department for Education and Employment. [Report].

Keywords: The Person

Summary: From research on the attributes of effective teaching and their major effect on student achievement, the author describes three characteristics of effective teaching under the control of teachers: teaching skills, professional characteristics, and classroom climate. Teaching skills and professional characteristics—skills teachers bring into the classroom—interact to create a classroom climate conducive to learning. No prescribed combination of skills and characteristics creates a particular classroom environment; instead, effective teachers contribute their individual combinations of skills and characteristics in multiple ways to create successful learning environments.

Effective teachers have extensive content knowledge and possess a bank of appropriate teaching strategies, which they apply to their knowledge of the ways in which students learn. Since effective teachers significantly influence student progress, these three characteristics form a foundation for professional development programs and underscore teacher impact on raising school standards. The article analyzes and discusses the characteristics and the various levels of each one to create a model of teacher effectiveness. The teachers' descriptions were based on the following items:

• Professionalism—challenge and support, confidence, creating trust, respect for others.

• Thinking—analytical thinking, conceptual thinking.

• Planning and setting expectations—drive for improvement, information seeking, initiative.

• Leading—flexibility, holding people accountable, managing pupils, passion for learning.

• Relating to others—impact and influence, working in teams, understanding others.

Miller, J. W., McKenna, M. C., & McKenna, B. A. (1998). A Comparison of Alternatively and Traditionally Prepared Teachers. *Journal of Teacher Education, 49*(3), 165–176. [Journal article].

Keywords: Prerequisites, Planning for Instruction

Summary: The study compares a traditional certification program with an alternative certification program. The 82 teachers in the study were matched by three years of experience and teaching assignment according to grade level, subject, and school. The investigation was divided into three studies.

• *Study 1: Teacher Performance.* No significant differences were found between the two groups in the area of pupil interaction or effective lessons.

• *Study 2: Student Achievement.* Fifth or sixth grade students in the teacher's self-contained classrooms for the entire year were assessed using pre-test and post-test scores earned on achievement tests. There were no significant differences on the pre-test or post-test scores using the Iowa Test of Basic Skills.

• *Study 3: Teacher Perception of Teaching Abilities.* Content analysis of teacher interviews found that neither group felt well-prepared to start teaching. While traditionally certified teachers attribute their feelings of unease to lack of teaching experience, the alternatively certified teachers attribute their lack of behavior management and instructional preparation skills to the gaps in their educational preparation.

The alternative program utilized in this study gives individuals with bachelor's degrees condensed coursework in pedagogy and a strong mentoring component with ongoing coursework during the first year of teaching. The study concluded that, after three years, there were no discernable differences in teacher effectiveness between traditionally prepared teachers and those prepared in the alternative program.

Monk, D. H., & King, J. A. (1994). Multilevel Teacher Resource Effects on Pupil Performance in Secondary Mathematics and Science: The Case of Teacher Subject-Matter Preparation. In R. G. Ehrenberg (Ed.), *Choices and Consequences: Contemporary Policy Issues in Education* (pp. 29–58). Ithaca, NY: ILR Press. [Book chapter].

Keywords: Prerequisites, The Person

Summary: This study examined the effect on academic achievement of the subject-matter knowledge of secondary math and science teachers. A survey determined the number of subject-related courses taken by teachers, and items from the National Assessment of Educational Progress (NAEP) measured student performance. The authors found the following results:

• An effective teacher influences a student's willingness to focus on subject matter; an ineffective teacher discourages student interest.

• Two students with comparable socioeconomic status and mathematics pre-test scores enrolled in different types of mathematics courses showed different gain scores, with the student in the more advanced course showing higher gains.

• The positive effect for students in advanced courses was not as great as the negative effect for students in remedial courses. However, students who scored low on pre-tests were positively affected by placement in advanced courses.

• Teacher subject-matter preparation was related more strongly to positive effects for students scoring high on pre-tests in the sophomore year of a two-year sequence. In the second year, the students who scored low on pre-tests showed stronger gains, possibly due to increased subject-matter coverage in math.

• In the sophomore year for students with low pre-test scores, teacher experience showed positive effects. These gains could be the result of increased coverage of curriculum or of the quality of teaching.

• Students with high pre-test scores in both mathematics and science were more likely to be assigned to teachers with more subject-matter preparation than students with low scores on the pre-test.

National Association of Secondary School Principals. (1997). Students Say: What Makes a Good Teacher? *Schools in the Middle, 6*(5), 15–17. [Journal article].

Keywords: Prerequisites, The Person, Implementing Instruction

Summary: This brief article outlines some of the results of a 1996 survey of almost 1,000 students between the ages of 13 and 17 who were asked to identify characteristics of best and worst teachers. The students responded that the number one characteristic of good teachers is their sense of humor. The number one characteristic of their worst teachers was that they are "dull and boring."

The following lists of the top five characteristics of the best and the worst teachers are a result of student responses to the survey. The top five characteristics of best teachers are that they have a sense of humor; make the class interesting; have knowledge of their subjects; explain things clearly; and spend time helping students. The top five characteristics of worst teachers are that they are dull or have a boring class; do not explain things clearly; show favoritism toward students; have a poor attitude; and expect too much from students.

Peart, N. A., & Campbell, F. A. (1999). At-Risk Students' Perceptions of Teacher Effectiveness. *Journal for a Just and Caring Education, 5*(3), 269–284. [Journal article].

Keywords: Prerequisites, The Person, Management and Organization, Planning for Instruction, Implementing Instruction, Monitoring Progress and Potential, Teachers of At-Risk Students

Summary: Teacher effectiveness was ranked fourth in factors affecting achievement of African American students, accompanied by cultural differences, minority status, and poverty. Forty-seven African American adults were interviewed about teacher characteristics that facilitate or inhibit school success. Four areas were identified as important for teachers to address in order to promote student achievement:

• *Interpersonal Skills.* A positive student-teacher relationship is developed by showing interest in students and demonstrating caring, concern, and empathy for them. One-on-one instruction is vital, as is teacher self-disclosure and availability.

• *Instructional Methods.* The ability to communicate the material effectively with genuine enthusiasm is essential. The teacher must have a command of the content and employ a bank of effective strategies for teaching it.

• *Motivational Leader.* The teacher who sets high standards for academic success, maintains an orderly environment, and encourages students to take responsibility for their learning should also assign appropriate challenges and offer reinforcement and encouragement.

• *Racial Impartiality.* Equitable treatment of all students is imperative. In addition, school activities must be inclusive of various cultures.

The academic success of at-risk students is enhanced if a personal connection that communicates respect and caring exists between the teacher and the student. The establishment of high academic expectations and a teacher's ability to enable students to meet the standards are important factors for positive perceptions of teacher effectiveness among African Americans.

Pressley, M., Raphael, L., Gallagher, J. D., & DiBella, J. (2004). Providence-St. Mel School: How a School That Works for African American Students Works. *Journal of Educational Psychology, 96*(2), 216–235. [Journal article].

Keywords: The Person, Implementing Instruction, Monitoring Progress and Potential, Teachers of At-Risk Students

Summary: Using qualitative methods, researchers studied one K–12 school in which urban minority students excel despite being located in one of the poorer areas of Chicago. Students must apply to attend the school, and parents must attend conferences and participate in the education of their children. The primary method of data collection was observation, in which observers would visit classes and report on artifacts and behaviors. A questionnaire relating to the reasons why the school was so effective was also administered to 362 students and 22 teachers. Documents including handbooks, regulations, standardized test summary data, and articles were analyzed. The researchers offer factors that emerged as essential to the culture of the school:

• *High Accountability.* Teachers constantly monitor the academic progress of students and intervene on an individual basis.

• *Total Academic Time.* Teachers greet students when they arrive for school and spend time in the cafeteria talking to students. They offer assistance before and after school.

• *The School Building.* Despite being located in an economically depressed area, the school is safe and clean, with space to accommodate technology labs, a library, a large auditorium, and a gymnasium.

• *Talented and Dedicated People Who Make It Work.* The administration and teachers dedicate themselves to seeing that their students succeed. Students and families were also seen as vital to the success of the school. Students describe their teachers as caring about them on a personal basis. Teachers make excellent use of class time, collaborate with colleagues, and maintain contact with families.

• *Instruction that Supports High and Meaningful Academic Achievement.* The school demands academic excellence and offers support to students. Teachers frequently administer tests to assess student progress and provide written feedback to students. They emphasize understandings rather than isolated facts, scaffold learning, and encourage students to take responsibility for their own learning.

Other factors that characterized the school include motivating students, preparing students for tests, mentoring for college admissions, and arranging events that support academic achievement. The researchers conclude that the school studied exhibits some of the factors already examined in school effectiveness research and exhibits some factors that are not emphasized in the research literature on school effectiveness.

Rowan, B., Chiang, F. S., & Miller, R. J. (1997). Using Research on Employees' Performance to Study the Effects of Teachers on Students' Achievement. *Sociology of Education, 70,* 256–284. [Journal article].

Keywords: Prerequisites, The Person

Summary: This article reports on a study that used the general perceptions about employees' performance to investigate the impact of teachers on student achievement. The study hypothesized that a teacher's effect on student achievement can be attributed to the variables of teacher ability, motivation, and work situation. Unlike previous research, this study examines the combined effect of these three variables on student achievement.

The study sample, consisting of 5,381 students at 382 public schools and 28 Catholic schools, was limited to students who had taken both the 8th and 10th grade National Education Longitudinal Study (NELS) of 1988 mathematics tests. The study controls for a large number of variables, including prior student achievement and students' opportunities to learn the content tested on the NELS mathematics test.

The study's findings suggest that although the effect size was small, the authors consider that there is "preliminary support for the broad hypothesis that teaching performance is a function" of these three dimensions. The authors attribute the small effect size and uneven results across the variables to unreliability in measurement.

The study suggests the effect of teacher ability on student achievement varies depending on context of the ability. Highly talented and motivated teachers have the greatest effect on student achievement. Talent was defined by three measures of teacher ability: content knowledge, training in the field, and use of instructional strategies. Teacher motivation was characterized by high expectations of self and of students.

Shellard, E., & Protheroe, N. (2000). Effective Teaching: How Do We Know It When We See It? *The Informed Educator Series.* **Arlington, VA: Educational Research Service. [Monograph].**

Keywords: Implementing Instruction

Summary: Specific teacher behaviors are the keys to creating engaged, learning-focused classroom environments that produce high-performing students. The monograph states that these productive behaviors can be taught, and in order to identify them, four case studies are examined. The major productive behaviors found in each study are as follows:

• *Study 1: Planning for Instruction.* High-performing teachers thoroughly plan and organize for instruction.

• *Study 2: Combining Instructional Strategies.* In the SAGE Program, characterized by small class size, rigorous academics, appropriate staff development, and community partnerships, higher-performing teachers use a combination of teacher-directed and student-directed instruction, individualized instruction for specific needs, and ongoing assessment.

• *Study 3: Differentiation of Instruction.* High-performing teachers emphasize critical thinking skills, individualized instruction to meet specific needs, and employment of appropriate teaching strategies and techniques for differing student populations. In this case study, teachers who use hands-on activities increased NAEP scores in science and math.

• *Study 4: Interactive Teaching Style.* Teachers who were interactive rather than didactic and spent a minimum of time reviewing past information have higher-achieving students. High-quality staff development was a major factor for those teachers who utilize interactive teaching methods.

The overview of the four studies indicates six behavioral characteristics of effective teachers: more time spent on academic tasks and strong classroom management; clear learning goals; students as active learners; individualized instruction to accommodate individual differences; combination of skills-based and higher-level instruction; and supportive and collaborative classroom climate.

A vital component for effective teaching is staff development that includes both modeling of the behaviors by master teachers and opportunities for observation and practice on the part of the teachers who desire to improve their classroom performance.

VanTassel-Baska, J., & Little, C. (Eds.). (2003). *Content-Based Curriculum for High-Ability Learners.* **Waco, TX: Prufrock Press. [Book].**

Keywords: Prerequisites, Management and Organization, Planning for Instruction, Implementing Instruction, Monitoring Progress and Potential, Teachers of High-Ability Students

Summary: The purpose of this book is to provide a framework for planning and implementing effective instruction for students with high abilities. The foundation for the book rests on the Integrated Curriculum Model (ICM), which consists of three interlocking dimensions. These dimensions include providing advanced content, focusing on higher-order processes and products, and selecting themes and issues that focus on connecting content with real-world implications. One of the important factors cited in successful implementation of the model is the teacher, specifically the training a teacher receives in how to teach gifted students. Section I of the book examines the use of acceleration, higher-order thinking skills, creativity, and concept development in achieving the goals of the curriculum model. Section II focuses on developing and implementing curriculum in each of the core subject areas: mathematics, science, language arts, and social studies. The final section looks at instructional actions important to implementing ICM. These include selecting appropriate materials, making instructional choices based on contextual factors, assessing student progress, and aligning curriculum for high-ability learners with content standards that already exist at the national, state, and local levels. In summary, the book stresses the importance of the teacher and the teacher's abilities in planning for and implementing instruction for gifted students.

Walsh, J. A., & Sattes, B. D. (2005). *Quality Questioning: Research-Based Practice to Engage Every Learner.* **Thousand Oaks, CA: Corwin Press. [Book].**

Keywords: Implementing Instruction

Summary: Adept use of questioning is a necessary part of the repertoire of effective teachers. The authors of this book examine the research behind effective questioning and offer characteristics of quality questioning as well as ways to increase student engagement through questioning. In a review of relevant literature, the authors summarized the research in six findings and provide implications for practice associated with those findings:

- Teachers ask a lot of questions.
- Most questions asked focus on factual knowledge.
- Not all students are involved in class discussions.
- Teachers neglect to provide adequate wait time.
- Teachers fail to probe students who respond with an incorrect answer.
- Teachers ask most of the questions in class, not students.

The authors frame the book and examine questioning within a professional development process model called Questioning and Understanding to Improve Learning and Thinking (QUILT). The model involves five stages: preparing the question; presenting the question; prompting student responses; processing student responses; and reflecting on questioning practices. The authors contend that following the five stages will lead to more effective questioning and addressing of research findings.

Wang, M. C., Haertel, G. D., & Walberg, H. J. (1993/1994, December/January). What Helps Students Learn? *Educational Leadership, 51*(4), 74–79. [Journal article].

Keywords: Management and Organization, Planning for Instruction, Implementing Instruction, Monitoring Progress and Potential

Summary: This meta-analysis of 331 sources results in 11,000 statistical findings that show consensus on the significant influences on learning. Direct influences, such as time spent teaching a specific topic, have more effect on student learning than indirect influences, such as policies. The findings are grouped into 28 categories and ranked by scholars. Of these categories, classroom management was determined to have the greatest impact on learning. However, when the categories are regrouped into six areas of influence, the weighting of the categories shows that student aptitude, classroom instruction and climate, and out-of-school contexts are approximately equal in their influence on learning.

Student aptitude is most influential in learning. This includes metacognitive and cognitive processes, social and behavioral attributes, motivational and affective attributes, and, to a lesser degree, the influence of psychomotor skills and student demographics. Classroom instruction and climate include the influences of social interactions between the teacher and student, quality of instruction, and the climate of the classroom environment.

Out-of-school contexts consider the home environment, community influences, and how time is spent outside of school. The instructional program design and the school organization affect learning to a lesser degree. The characteristics of individual states and districts have the least effect on learning as they are quite removed from the actual classroom environment. By aligning classroom practices with state and district policies and the other areas of influence, a more effective route to reform can be established.

Weiss, I. R., & Pasley, J. D. (2004). What Is High-Quality Instruction? *Educational Leadership, 61*(5), 24–28. [Journal article].

Keywords: Implementing Instruction, Teachers of At-Risk Students

Summary: The authors of this article report on research conducted over a year and a half in which more than 350 mathematics and science lessons were observed, analyzed, and followed up with interviews in order to examine the decisions that teachers make on a daily, even minute-by-minute, basis. The lessons were observed using the following indicators: quality of content, quality of implementation, and classroom culture. Overall, the researchers found that mathematics and science education were lacking in rigor and in teaching excellence. However, the content taught was accurate and worthwhile. Lessons were divided into very effective and very ineffective. Those that were effective were characterized in the following ways:

• Teachers used a variety of instructional activities to engage students with worthwhile content.

• The classroom climate was both rigorous and respectful.

• Teachers engaged all students in the lesson, not just volunteers.

• Teachers used questioning to help students create meaningful understandings of new concepts.

• Teachers provided explanations at appropriate times in the lesson to further student understandings.

Based on their research, the authors suggest the following strategies to improve mathematics and science instruction:

• Develop lesson study groups to analyze and discuss lesson implementation.

• Adopt and use instructional resources that provide specific assistance to teachers.

• Develop and implement professional development that mirrors elements of high-quality instruction.

• Resolve unequal access to education.

• Align policies among school, district, and state levels.

Wenglinsky, H. (2004). Closing the Racial Achievement Gap: The Role of Reforming Instructional Practices. *Education Policy Analysis Archives, 12*(64). [Online journal article]. Available: http://epaa.asu.edu/epaa/v12n64

Keywords: Implementing Instruction, Monitoring Progress and Potential, Teachers of At-Risk Students

Summary: Instructional practices are at the center of studying the achievement gap in this research study. The NAEP mathematics results from 13,511 4th graders and student and teacher questionnaire data were used to develop a model of student achievement at both the student and school levels. The purpose of the study was to determine whether instructional practices had an impact on achievement gaps, focusing on gaps between schools or between classrooms within one school. Another purpose of this study was to determine which instructional practices contributed most to closing achievement gaps. The researchers concluded that instructional practices mostly affect achievement from classroom to classroom but not from school to school. Second, effective instructional practices are specific to topics covered in class. Practices that were beneficial for all students included increased time on task, routine mathematics exercises, and an emphasis on geometry. Practices that had overall negative effects included frequent testing and emphasis on isolated facts over conceptual understandings.

Westberg, K., & Archambault, F. (1997, Winter). A Multi-Site Case Study of Successful Classroom Practices for High Ability Students. *Gifted Child Quarterly, 41*(1), 42–51. [Journal article].

Keywords: Prerequisites, Planning for Instruction, Implementing Instruction, Teachers of High-Ability Students

Summary: This study of classroom practices employed a qualitative research design in which researchers observed classrooms, conducted interviews, and reviewed school documents related to gifted instruction. Ten elementary school sites were selected based on recommendations by state and local education officials as to which schools were particularly adept at meeting the needs of high-ability students. From the observations, interviews, and document analyses, six themes emerged:

• *Teachers' Advanced Training and Knowledge.* Teachers at these effective schools had either pursued advanced education to meet the needs of highly able learners or they had attended professional development classes. They were described as lifelong learners who were interested in finding new ways to improve education in their own classrooms.

• *Teachers' Willingness and Readiness to Embrace Change.* The teachers were willing to try new strategies, even at the risk of failure. They continually sought ways to change and improve.

• *Collaboration.* Teachers collaborated within their grade levels, with gifted specialists, and with curriculum specialists. The teachers in these schools were provided the time to collaborate, which the researchers contend was a critical element to being able to collaborate.

• *Teachers' Beliefs and Strategies for Differentiating Instruction.* Teachers were aware that students learn in different ways and at differing paces. Therefore, teachers used a variety of activities and individualized instruction to meet the needs of the students in the classroom.

• *Leadership.* Educational leaders such as superintendents and principals supported and advocated programs for high-ability students.

• *Autonomy and Support.* Teachers felt that they had both the support of the school leaders and the autonomy to implement new strategies in the classroom. They did not feel threatened if a strategy failed.

The authors contend that these six themes are indicative of successful classroom practices at the 10 elementary school sites studied. The authors further state that the truly effective teacher plans and implements instruction to accommodate both the similarities and differences among students in the classroom.

Willard-Holt, C. (2003). Raising Expectations for the Gifted. *Educational Leadership, 61*(2), 72–75. [Journal article].

Keywords: Implementing Instruction, Monitoring Progress and Potential, Teachers of High-Ability Students

Summary: Teaching high-ability or gifted learners in the regular education classroom can be a challenge. The key to meeting this challenge is differentiation in the classroom. This article details five strategies to address the needs of those students who may become bored in a regular educational setting. Another key to differentiation in the classroom is the teacher's ability to assess what the students already know and are able to do. Only after such assessment can differentiation take place. The five strategies discussed include the following:

• *Curriculum Compacting.* Assess what students know prior to a unit of study and eliminate content or skills that have been mastered.

• *Flexible Grouping.* Use both heterogeneous and homogeneous grouping within a unit of study.

• *Product Choices.* Allow students to choose how they will demonstrate their mastery of content and skills.

• *Multilevel Learning Stations.* Provide stations for students to conduct independent work that span the levels of Bloom's taxonomy of thinking.

• *Inspiring Extraordinary Achievement.* Develop individual education plans for students who are at a highly advanced level.

The author suggests that these strategies can assist a teacher in meeting the needs of gifted students in the regular education classroom through differentiation of instruction.

Williams, B. (2003). *Closing the Achievement Gap: A Vision for Changing Beliefs and Practices* **(2nd ed.). Alexandria, VA: Association for Supervision and Curriculum Development. [Book].**

Keywords: Prerequisites, The Person, Implementing Instruction, Monitoring Progress and Potential, Teachers of At-Risk Students

Summary: This book focuses on answering the question, "What else do we need to know and do to close the achievement gaps among groups?" Throughout the nine chapters, the authors seek to further examine individual differences, the nature of the achievement gap, and strategies that not only narrow but close the gaps that exist. The teacher is a central element, as most of the chapters focus on an aspect of effective teachers. The editor identifies state and federal legislators, educators, institutions that prepare teachers, community and parent leaders, and education researchers as the target audience for the book.

References

Adams, C. R., & Singh, K. (1998). Direct and indirect effects of school learning variables on the academic achievement of African American 10th graders. *The Journal of Negro Education, 67*(1), 48–66.

Agne, K. J. (1992). Caring: The expert teacher's edge. *Educational Horizons, 70*(3), 120–124.

Agne, K. J. (2001). Gifted: The lost minority. *Kappa Delta Pi Record, 37*(4), 168–172.

Allington, R. L. (2002). What I've learned about effective reading instruction. *Phi Delta Kappan, 83,* 740–747.

Andrew, M., Cobb, C., & Giampietro, P. (2005). Verbal ability and teacher effectiveness. *Journal of Teacher Education, 56*(4), 343–354.

Archer, J. (1998). *Students' fortunes rest with assigned teacher.* Retrieved August 21, 2006, from www.edweek.org/ew/1998/23dallas.h17.

Armor, D., Contry-Oseguera, P., Cox, M., King, N., McDonnell, M., Pascal, A., et al. (1976). *Analysis of school preferred reading program in selected Los Angeles minority schools.* Santa Monica, CA: RAND.

Ashton, P., & Crocker, L. (1987). Systematic study of planned variations: The essential focus of teacher education reform. *Journal of Teacher Education, 38,* 2–8.

Astor, R. A., Meyer, H. A., & Behre, W. J. (1999). Unowned places and times: Maps and interviews about violence in high schools. *American Educational Research Journal, 36*(1), 3–42.

Bain, H. P., & Jacobs, R. (1990, September). The case for smaller classes and better teachers. *Streamlined Seminar—National Association of Elementary School Principals, 9*(1).

Baker, J. A. (1999). Teacher-student interaction in urban at-risk classrooms: Differential behavior, relationship quality, and student satisfaction. *The Elementary School Journal, 100*(1), 57–70.

Bangert-Downs, R. L., Kulik, C. C., Kulick, J. A., & Morgan, M. (1991). The instructional effects of feedback in test-like events. *Review of Educational Research, 61*(2), 213–54.

Barton, P. E. (2003). *Parsing the achievement gap: Baselines for tracking progress.* Princeton, NJ: Educational Testing Service. Retrieved August 21, 2006, from www.ets.org/research/pic/parsing.pdf.

Baska, L. K. (1989). Characteristics and needs of the gifted. In J. Feldhusen, J. VanTassel-Baska, & K. Seeley (Eds.), *Excellence in educating the gifted* (pp. 15–28). Denver, CO: Love Publishing.

Battle-Bailey, L. (2003). *Training teachers to design interactive homework. ERIC Digest.* Washington, DC: ERIC Clearinghouse on Teaching and Teacher Education. (ERIC Document Reproduction Service No. ED 482 700).

Begle, E. G. (1979). *Critical variables in mathematics education: Findings from a survey of the empirical literature.* Washington, DC: National Council of Teachers of Mathematics.

Belton, L. (1996, September). What our teachers should know and be able to do: A student's view. *Educational Leadership, 54*(1), 66–68.

Bennett, A., Bridglall, B., Cauce, A., Everson, H., Gordon, E., Lee, C., Mendoza-Denton, R., Renzulli, J., & Steward, J. (2004). *All students reaching the top: Strategies for closing academic achievement gaps.* Available: www.ncrel.org/gap/studies/thetop.htm.

Berendt, P. R., & Koski, B. (1999, March). No shortcuts to success. *Educational Leadership, 56*(6), 45–47.

Berliner, D. C. (1986). In pursuit of the expert pedagogue. *Educational Researcher, 15*(7), 5–13.

Berliner, D. C., & Rosenshine, B. V. (1977). The acquisition of knowledge in the classroom. In R. C. Anderson, R. J. Spiro, & W. E. Montague (Eds.), *Schooling and the acquisition of knowledge* (pp. 375–396). Hillsdale, NJ: Lawrence Erlbaum Associates.

Bernal, E. M. (1994). *Finding and cultivating minority gifted/talented students.* Paper presented at the National Conference on Alternative Teacher Certification, Washington, DC.

Bernard, B. (2003). Turnaround teachers and schools. In B. Williams (Ed.), *Closing the achievement gap: A vision for changing beliefs and practices* (pp. 115–137). Alexandria, VA: Association for Supervision and Curriculum Development.

Betts, J. R., Rueben, K. S., & Danenberg, A. (2000). *Equal resources, equal outcomes? The distribution of school resources and student achievement in California.* San Francisco: Public Policy Institute of California.

Black, P., Harrison, C., Lee, C., Marshall, B., & William, D. (2004). Working inside the black box: Assessment for learning in the classroom. *Phi Delta Kappan, 86*(1), 9–21.

Black, P., & William, D. (1998). Inside the black box: Raising standards through classroom assessment. *Phi Delta Kappan, 80*(2), 139–148.

Blair, J. (2000). ETS study links effective teaching methods to test-score gains. *Education Week, 20*(8), 24.

Bloom, B. S. (1984, May). The search for methods of group instruction as effective as one-to-one tutoring. *Educational Leadership, 41*(8), 4–17.

Bloom, B. S. (Ed.). (1985). *Developing talent in young people.* New York: Ballantine.

Bonesronning, H. (2004). Do the teachers' grading practices affect student achievement? *Education Economics, 12*(2), 151–168.

Borko, H., & Livingston, C. (1989). Cognition and improvisation: Differences in mathematics instruction by expert and novice teachers. *American Educational Research Journal, 26*(4), 473–498.

Boyd, D., Lankford, H., Loeb, S., & Wycoff, J. (2005). The draw of home: How teachers' preferences for proximity disadvantage urban schools. *Journal of Policy Analysis and Management, 24*(1), 113–132.

Boyle-Baise, M. (2005). Preparing community-oriented teachers: Reflections from a multicultural service-learning project. *Journal of Teacher Education, 56*(5), 446–458.

Bradford, D. (1999). Exemplary urban middle school teachers' use of 5 standards of effective teaching. *Teaching and Change, 7*(1), 53–78.

Brainard, S. G., & Carlin, L. (2001). A six-year longitudinal study of undergraduate women in engineering and science. In M. Lederman & I. Bartsch (Eds.), *The gender and science reader* (pp. 24–37). New York: Routledge.

Bratton, S. E. (1998). How we're using value-added assessment. *The School Administrator, 55*(11), 30–32.

Bridglall, B. L., & Gordon, E. W. (2003). *Raising minority achievement: The Department of Defense model. ERIC Digest.* New York: ERIC Clearinghouse on Urban Education, Institute for Urban and Minority Education. (ERIC Document Reproduction Service No. ED 480 919)

Brookhart, S. M., & Loadman, W. E. (1992). Teacher assessment and validity: What do we want to know? *Journal of Personnel Evaluation in Education, 5,* 347–357.

Brophy, J., & Good, T. L. (1986). Teacher behavior and student achievement. In M. C. Wittrock (Ed.), *Handbook of research on teaching* (3rd ed., pp. 328–371). New York: Macmillan.

Brophy, J. E., & Good, T. L. (1997). *Looking into classrooms.* New York: Longman.

Buttram, J. L., & Waters, J. T. (1997). Improving America's schools through standards-based education. *NASSP Bulletin, 81*(590), 1–5.

Callahan, C. M. (2001, November). Beyond the gifted stereotype. *Educational Leadership, 59*(3), 42–46.

Carlsen, W. S. (1987). *Why do you ask? The effects of science teacher subject matter knowledge on teacher questioning and classroom discourse.* Paper presented at the annual meeting of the American Educational Research Association, Washington, DC.

Carlsen, W. S., & Wilson, S. M. (1988, April). *Responding to student questions: The effects of teacher subject matter knowledge and experience on teacher discourse strategies.* Paper presented at the annual meeting of the American Educational Research Association, Washington, DC.

Carper, A. (2002). *Bright students in a wasteland: The at-risk gifted: A qualitative study of fourteen gifted dropouts.* Unpublished doctoral dissertation, North Carolina State University.

Carroll, J. M. (1994). *The Copernican plan evaluated: The evolution of a revolution.* Topsfield, MA: Copernican Associates.

Cavalluzzo, L. C. (2004). *Is National Board certification an effective signal of teacher quality?* Alexandria, VA: The CAN Corporation. Retrieved August 21, 2006, from www.cna.org/documents/cavaluzzostudy.pdf.

Cawelti, G. (1999). *Portraits of six benchmark schools: Diverse approaches to improving student achievement.* Arlington, VA: Educational Research Service.

Cawelti, G. (Ed.). (2004). *Handbook of research on improving student achievement* (3rd ed.). Arlington, VA: Educational Research Service.

Chappius, S., & Stiggins, R. J. (2002, September). Classroom assessment for learning. *Educational Leadership, 60*(1), 40–43.

Christenson, S. L., & Sheridan, S. M. (2001). *Schools and families: Creating essential connections for learning.* New York: Guilford Press.

The Civil Rights Project, Harvard University. (2005). *Confronting the graduation crisis in California.* Retrieved on August 21, 2006, from www.civilrightsproject.harvard.edu/research/dropouts/dropouts05.pdf.

Clare, L. (2000). *Using teachers' assignments as an indicator of classroom practice* (CSE Technical Report). Los Angeles: Center for Research and Evaluation, Standards, and Student Testing.

Cline, S., & Schwartz, D. (1999). *Diverse populations of gifted children: Meeting their needs in the regular classroom and beyond.* Upper Saddle River, NJ: Merrill.

Clotfelter, C. T., Ladd, H. F., & Vigdor, J. (2005). Who teaches whom? Race and the distribution of novice teachers. *Economics of Education Review, 24*(4), 377–392.

Clotfelter, C. T., Ladd, H. F., Vigdor, J. L., & Diaz, R. A. (2004). Do school accountability systems make it more difficult for low-performing schools to attract and retain high-quality teachers? *Journal of Policy Analysis and Management, 23*(2), 251–271.

Clubine, B., Knight, D. L., Schneider, C. L., & Smith, P. A. (2001). *Opening doors: Promising lessons from five Texas high schools.* Austin, TX: Charles A. Dana Center, The University of Texas.

Colangelo, N., Assouline, S. G., & Gross, M. U. M. (Eds.). (2004). *A nation deceived: How schools hold back America's brightest students: The Templeton national report on acceleration* (Vol. 1). Iowa City, IA: The Connie Belin & Jacqueline N. Blank International Center for Gifted Education and Talent Development.

Colangelo, N., Assouline, S. G., & Lupkowski-Shoplik, A. E. (2004). Whole-grade acceleration. In N. Colangelo, S. G. Assouline, & M. U. M. Gross (Eds.), *A nation deceived: How schools hold back America's brightest students: The Templeton national report on acceleration* (Vol. 2, pp. 77–86). Iowa City, IA: The Connie Belin & Jacqueline N. Blank International Center for Gifted Education and Talent Development.

Coleman, J. S., Campbell, E. Q., Hobson, C. J., McPartland, J., Mood, A. M., Weinfield, F. D., et al. (1966). *Equality of educational opportunity.* Washington, DC: U.S. Government Printing Office.

Collinson, V., Killeavy, M., & Stephenson, H. J. (1999). Exemplary teachers: Practicing an ethic of care in England, Ireland, and the United States. *Journal for a Just and Caring Education, 5*(4), 349–366.

Cooper, H., Jackson, K., Nye, B., & Lindsay, J. J. (2001). A model of homework's influence on the performance evaluations of elementary students. *The Journal of Experimental Education, 69*(2), 181–191.

Cooper, H., Lindsay, J. J., Nye, B., & Greathouse, S. (1998). Relationships among attitudes about homework, amount of homework assigned and completed, and student achievement. *Journal of Educational Psychology, 90*(1), 70–83.

Copenhaver, R. W., & McIntyre, D. J. (1992). Teachers' perception of gifted students. *Roeper Review, 14,* 151–153.

Corbett, D., & Wilson, B. (2002, September). What urban students say about good teaching. *Educational Leadership, 60*(1), 18–22.

Cotton, K. (1999). *Research you can use to improve results.* Portland, OR: Northwest Regional Educational Laboratory; and Alexandria, VA: Association for Supervision and Curriculum Development.

Cotton, K. (2000). *The schooling practices that matter most.* Portland, OR: Northwest Regional Educational Laboratory; and Alexandria, VA: Association for Supervision and Curriculum Development.

Coulter, F. (1985). Homework. In T. Husen & T. N. Postlethwaite (Eds.), *The international encyclopedia of education: Research and studies* (pp. 2289–2294). New York: Pergamon Press.

Covino, E. A., & Iwanicki, E. (1996). Experienced teachers: Their constructs on effective teaching. *Journal of Personnel Evaluation in Education, 11,* 325–363.

Cox, J., Daniel, N., & Boston, B. O. (1985). *Educating able learners: Programs and promising practices.* Austin, TX: University of Texas Press.

Cruickshank, D. R., & Haefele, D. (2001, February). Good teachers, plural. *Educational Leadership, 58*(5), 26–30.

Csikszentmihalyi, M., Rathunde, K., & Whalen, S. (1993). *Talented teenagers: The roots of success and failure.* New York: Cambridge University Press.

Cunningham, P. M., & Allington, R. L. (1999). *Classrooms that work: They can all read and write.* New York: Longman.

Danielson, C. (2002). *Enhancing student achievement: A framework for school improvement.* Alexandria, VA: Association for Supervision and Curriculum Development.

Darling-Hammond, L. (1996). What matters most: A competent teacher for every child. *Phi Delta Kappan, 78*(3), 193–200.

Darling-Hammond, L. (2000). *Teacher quality and student achievement: A review of state policy evidence.* Retrieved August 21, 2006, from http://epaa.asu.edu/epaa/v8n1/.

Darling-Hammond, L. (2001, February). The challenge of staffing our schools. *Educational Leadership, 58*(8), 12–17.

Darling-Hammond, L., Berry, B., & Thoreson, A. (2001). Does teacher certification matter? Evaluating the evidence. *Educational Evaluation and Policy Analysis, 23*(1), 57–77.

Darling-Hammond, L., Holtzman, D. J., Gatlin, S. J., & Heilig, J. V. (2005). Does teacher preparation matter? Evidence about teacher certification, Teach for America, and teacher effectiveness. *Education Policy Analysis Archives, 13*(42). Retrieved August 21, 2006, from http://epaa.asu.edu/epaa/v13n42/.

Darling-Hammond, L., & Sykes, G. (2003). Wanted: A national teacher supply policy for education: The right way to meet the "highly qualified teacher" challenge? *Education Policy Analysis Archives, 11*(33). Retrieved August 21, 2006, from http://epaa.asu.edu/epaa/v11n33/.

Day, S. L. (2002). Real kids, real risks: Effective instruction of students at risk of failure. *NASSP Bulletin, 86*(682). Retrieved August 21, 2006, from www.principals.org/news/bultn_realkids0902.html.

Demmon-Berger, D. (1986). *Effective teaching: Observations from research.* Arlington, VA: American Association of School Administrators.

Donovan, M. S., Bransford, J. D., & Pellegrino, J. W. (1999). *How people learn: Bridging research and practice.* Washington, DC: National Academy Press.

Doyle, W. (1986). Classroom organization and management. In M. C. Wittrock (Ed.), *Handbook of research on teaching* (3rd ed., pp. 392–431). New York: Macmillan.

Dozier, T., & Bertotti, C. (2000). *Eliminating barriers to quality teaching.* Retrieved on August 21, 2006, from www.ed.gov/teacherquality/awareness.html.

Drummond, K. V., & Stipek, D. (2004). Low-income parents' beliefs about their role in academic learning. *The Elementary School Journal, 104*(3), 197–215.

Druva, C., & Anderson, R. D. (1983). Science teacher characteristics by teacher behavior and by student outcome: A meta-analysis of research. *Journal of Research in Science Teaching, 20*, 467–479.

Dubner, F. S. (1979). Thirteen ways of looking at a gifted teacher. *Journal for the Education of the Gifted, 3*(3), 143–146.

Dunkin, M. J. (1978). Student characteristics, classroom processes, and student achievement. *Journal of Educational Psychology, 70*, 998–1009.

Dunkin, M. J., & Doenau, S. J. (1980). A replication study of unique and joint contributions to variance in student achievement. *Journal of Educational Psychology, 72*(3), 394–403.

Education Review Office. (1998). *The capable teacher.* Retrieved August 21, 2006, from www.ero.govt.nz/ero/publishing.nsf/Content/The%20Capable%20Teacher.

Education USA Special Report. (n.d.). *Good teachers: What to look for.* Arlington, VA: National School Public Relations Association.

Educational Research Service. (2000). *Effective Classrooms: Teacher behaviors that produce high student achievement.* Arlington, VA: Author.

Eisner, E. W. (2003/2004, December/January). Preparing for today and tomorrow. *Educational Leadership, 61*(4), 6–10.

Emerick, L. J. (1992). Academic underachievement among the gifted: Students' perceptions of factors that reverse the pattern. *Gifted Child Quarterly, 36*(3), 140–146.

Emmer, E. T., Evertson, C. M., & Anderson, L. M. (1980). Effective classroom management at the beginning of the school year. *The Elementary School Journal, 80*(5), 219–231.

Emmer, E. T., Evertson, C. M., & Worsham, M. E. (2003). *Classroom management for secondary teachers.* Boston: Allyn and Bacon.

Esch, C. E., Chang-Ross, C. M., Guha, R., Humphrey, D. C., Shields, P. M., Tiffany-Morales, J. et al. (2005). *The status of the teaching profession 2005.* Santa Cruz, CA: The Center for the Future of Teaching and Learning.

Esch, C. E., Chang-Ross, C. M., Tiffany-Morales, J., & Shields, P. M. (2004). *California's teaching force: Key issues and trends.* Santa Cruz, CA: The Center for the Future of Teaching and Learning. Available: www.cftl.org/documents/2004/1204report/1204fullreport.pdf.

Eyre, D., Coates, D., Fitzpatrick, M., Higgins, C., McClure, L., Wilson, H., et al. (2002). Effective teaching of able pupils in primary school: The findings of the Oxfordshire effective teachers of able pupils project. *Gifted Education International, 16*(2), 158–162.

Feldhusen, J. F. (1991, September/October). Full-time classes for gifted youth. *Gifted Child Today, 14*(5), 10–13.

Feldhusen, J. F. (1997). Educating teachers for work with talented youth. In N. Colangelo & G. A. Davis (Eds.), *Handbook of gifted education* (2nd ed., pp. 547–552). Boston: Allyn and Bacon.

Feldhusen, J., VanTassel-Baska, J., & Seeley, K. (1989). *Excellence in teaching the gifted.* Denver, CO: Love Publishing.

Ferguson, P., & Womack, S. T. (1993). The impact of subject matter and education coursework on teaching performance. *Journal of Teacher Education, 44*(1), 55–63.

Ferguson, R. F. (1991). Paying for public education: New evidence on how and why money matters. *Harvard Journal on Legislation, 28,* 465–498.

Ferguson, R. F. (2002). *What doesn't meet the eye: Understanding and addressing racial disparities in high-achieving suburban schools.* Cambridge, MA: Harvard University Press.

Fetler, M. (1999). High school staff characteristics and mathematics test results. *Educational Policy Analysis Archives, 7*(9). Retrieved August 21, 2006, from http://epaa.asu.edu/epaa/v7n9.html.

Fidler, P. (2002). *The relationship between teacher instructional techniques and characteristics and student achievement in reduced size classes.* Los Angeles, CA: Los Angeles Unified School District.

Ford, D. Y., & Trotman, M. F. (2001). Teachers of gifted students: Suggested multicultural characteristics and competences. *Roeper Review, 23*(4), 235–239.

Freel, A. (1998, September). Achievement in urban schools: What makes the difference? *The Education Digest, 64*(1) 17–22.

Fuchs, L. S., Fuchs, D., & Phillips, N. (1994). The relation between teachers' beliefs about the importance of good work habits, teacher planning, and student achievement. *The Elementary School Journal, 94*(3), 331–345.

Fullerton, S. (2002). *Student engagement with schools: Individual and school-level influences.* (Research Report No. 27). Victoria, Australia: Australian Council for Educational Research.

Gardner, H. (1983). *Frames of mind.* New York: Basic Books.

Gitomer, D. H., Latham, A. S., & Ziomek, R. (1999). *The academic quality of prospective teachers: The impact of admissions and licensure testing.* Princeton, NJ: Educational Testing Service.

Goe, L. (2002). Legislating equity: The distribution of emergency permit teachers in California. *Education Policy Analysis Archives, 10*(42). Retrieved August 21, 2006, from http://epaa.asu.edu/epaa/v10n42.

Goldhaber, D., & Anthony, E. (2004, March). Can teacher quality be effectively assessed? Urban Institute. Retrieved August 21, 2006, from www.urban.org/url.cfm?ID=410958.

Goldhaber, D. D., & Brewer, D. J. (2000). Does teacher certification matter? High school teacher certification status and student achievement. *Educational Evaluation and Policy Analysis, 22*(2), 129–145.

Gonzalez, A. R. (2002). Parental involvement: Its contribution to high school students' motivation. *The Clearing House, 75*(3), 132–135.

Good, T. L., & Brophy, J. E. (1997). *Looking in classrooms* (7th ed.). New York: Addison-Wesley.

Good, T. L., & McCaslin, M. M. (1992). Teacher licensure and certification. In M. C. Alkin (Ed.), *Encyclopedia of educational research* (6th ed., pp. 1352–1388). New York: Macmillan.

Grant, B. (2002). Looking through the glasses: J. D. Salinger's wise children and gifted education. *Gifted Child Quarterly, 46*(1), 6–14.

Hamre, B. K., & Pianta, R. C. (2005). Can instructional and emotional support in the first-grade classroom make a difference for children at risk of school failure? *Child Development, 76*(5), 949–967.

Hansen, J., & Feldhusen, J. F. (1994). Comparison of trained and untrained teachers of gifted students. *Gifted Child Quarterly, 38*(3), 115–123.

Hanushek, E. (1971). Teacher characteristics and gains in student achievement: Estimation using micro data. *American Economic Review, 61*(2), 280–288.

Hawk, P. P., Coble, C. R., & Swanson, M. (1985). Certification: It does matter. *Journal of Teacher Education, 36*(3), 13–15.

Haycock, K. (2000). No more settling for less. *Thinking K–16, 4*(1), 3–12.

Haycock, K. (2003/2004, December/January). Toward a fair distribution of teacher talent. *Educational Leadership, 60*(4), 11–15.

Heath, W. J. (1997, May). *What are the most effective characteristics of teachers of the gifted?* (ERIC Document Reproduction Service No. ED 411 665).

Henderson, J. (1996). Effective teaching in advanced placement classrooms. *Journal of Classroom Instruction, 31*(1), 29–35.

Heritage, M., & Chen, E. (2005). Why data skills matter in school improvement. *Phi Delta Kappan, 86*(9), 707.

Hiebert, J., Stigler, J. W., Jacobs, J. K., Givvin, K. B., Garnier, H., Smith, M., et al. (2005). Mathematics teaching in the United States today (and tomorrow): Results from the TIMSS 1999 video study. *Educational Evaluation and Policy Analysis, 27*(2), 111–132.

Hill, H. C., Rowan, B., & Ball, D. L. (2005). Effects of teachers' mathematical knowledge for teaching on student achievement. *American Educational Research Journal, 42*(2), 371–406.

Ho Sui-Chu, E., & Willms, J. D. (1996). Effects of parental involvement on eighth grade achievement. *Sociology of Education, 69*(2), 126–141.

Hoff, D. J. (2003, Sep 3). Large scale study finds poor math science instruction. *Education Week, 23*(1), 8.

Hoffman, D., & Levak, B. A. (2003, September). Personalizing schools. *Educational Leadership, 61*(1), 30–34.

Holloway, J. H. (2003, October). Research link: Grouping gifted students. *Educational Leadership, 61*(2), 89–91.

Holt-Reynolds, D. (1999). Good readers, good teachers? Subject matter expertise as a challenge in learning to teach. *Harvard Educational Review, 69*(1), 29–50.

Howard, T. C. (2002). Hearing footsteps in the dark: African-American students' descriptions of effective teachers. *Journal of Education for Students Placed at Risk, 4*(4), 425–444.

Hunt, B., & Seney, R. W. (2001). Planning the learning environment. In F. A. Karnes & S. M. Bean (Eds.), *Methods and materials for teaching the gifted and talented* (pp. 43–89). Waco, TX: Prufrock Press.

Hutchinson, L. (2004). *Recommended practices for effective teaching in the International Baccalaureate Program: An examination of instructional skills, assessment practices, and teacher-efficacy beliefs of IB teachers.* Unpublished doctoral dissertation, The College of William and Mary, Williamsburg, Virginia.

Ilmer, S., Snyder, J., Erbaugh, S., & Kurtz, K. (1997). Urban educators' perceptions of successful teaching. *Journal of Teacher Education, 48*(2), 379–384.

Ingersoll, R. M. (2001, May). The realities of out-of-field teaching. *Educational Leadership, 58*(8), 42–45.

Jackson, A. W., & Davis, G. A. (2000). *Turning points 2000: Educating adolescents in the 21st century.* New York: Teachers College Press.

Janisch, C., & Johnson, M. (2003). Effective literacy practices and challenging curriculum for at-risk learners: Great expectations. *Journal of Education for Students Placed at Risk, 8*(1), 295.

Jay, J. K. (2002). Points on a continuum: An expert/novice study of pedagogical reasoning. *The Professional Educator, 24*(2), 63–74.

Johnsen, S. K., Haensley, P., Ryser, G., & Ford, R. (2002). Changing general education classroom practices to adapt for gifted students. *Gifted Child Quarterly, 46*(1), 45–63.

Johnsen, S. K., & Ryser, G. R. (1996). An overview of effective practices with gifted students in general education settings. *Journal for the Education of the Gifted, 19*(4), 379–405.

Johnson, B. L. (1997). An organizational analysis of multiple perspectives of effective teaching: Implications for teacher evaluation. *Journal of Personnel Evaluation in Education, 11,* 69–87.

Johnson, D. (2000). *Teaching mathematics to gifted students in a mixed-ability classroom. ERIC EC digest #E594.* Retrieved August 21, 2006, from http://ericec.org/digests/c594.html.

Johnson, J. (2004, May). What school leaders want. *Educational Leadership, 61*(7), 24–27.

Johnson, S. M., Birkeland, S. E., & Peske, H. G. (2005). Life in the fast track: How states seek to balance incentives and quality in alternative teacher certification programs. *Educational Policy, 19*(1), 63–89.

Kain, J. F., & Singleton, K. (1996, May/June). Equality of educational opportunity revisited. *New England Economic Review,* 87–114.

Kane, T. J., Rockoff, J. E., & Staiger, D. O. (2006, April). *What does teacher certification tell us about teacher effectiveness? Evidence from New York City.* (Working Paper No. 12155). New York: National Bureau of Economic Research.

Karnes, F. A., & Bean, S. M. (Eds.). (2001). *Methods and materials for teaching the gifted and talented.* Waco, TX: Prufrock Press.

Keith, T. Z., Reimers, T. M., Fehrmann, P. G., Pottebaum, S. M., & Aubey, L. W. (1986). Parental involvement, homework, and TV time: Direct and indirect effects on high school achievement. *Journal of Educational Psychology, 78*(5), 373–380.

Kerrins, J. A., & Cushing, K. S. (1998). *Taking a second look: Expert and novice differences when observing the same classroom teaching segment a second time.* Paper presented at the annual meeting of the American Educational Research Association, San Diego, CA.

Knapp, M. S., Shields, P. M., & Turnbull, B. J. (1992). *Academic challenge for the children of poverty: Summary report.* Washington, DC: U.S. Department of Education, Office of Policy and Planning.

Kober, N. (2001). *It takes more than testing: Closing the achievement gap.* Washington, DC: Center on Education Policy. Retrieved August 21, 2006, from www.ctredpol.org/improvingpublicschools/closingachievementgap.pdf.

Kohn, A. (1996, September). What to look for in a classroom. *Educational Leadership, 54*(1), 54–55.

Kounin, J. (1970). *Discipline and group management in classrooms.* New York: Holt, Rinehart, & Winston.

Kozol, J. (2005, September). Still separate, still unequal. *Harper's Magazine,* 41–54.

Kulik, J. A., & Kulik, C. L. C. (1992). Meta-analytic findings on grouping programs. *Gifted Child Quarterly, 36,* 73–77.

Laczko-Kerr, I., & Berliner, D. (2002). The effectiveness of Teach for America and other under-certified teachers on student academic achievement: A case of harmful public policy. *Educational Policy Analysis Archives, 10*(37). Retrieved August 21, 2006, from http://epaa.asu/edu/epaa/v10n37.

Langer, J. A. (2000). Excellence in English in middle and high school: How teachers' professional lives support student achievement. *American Educational Research Journal, 37*(2), 397–439.

Langer, J. (2001). Beating the odds: Teaching middle and high school students to read and write well. *American Educational Research Journal, 38*(4), 837–880.

Lee-Corbin, H., & Denicolo, P. (1998, December). Portraits of the able child: Highlights of case study research. *High Ability Studies, 9*(2), 207–219.

Lewis, A. (with Paik, S.). (2001). Add it up: Using research to improve education for low-income and minority students. Washington, DC: Poverty & Race Research Action Council. Retrieved August 21, 2006, from www.prrac.org/pubs_aiu.pdf.

Lilly, M. S. (1992). Research on teacher licensure and state approval of teacher education programs. *Teacher Education and Special Education, 15,* 149–160.

Littky, D., & Grabelle, S. (2002). *The big picture: Education is everyone's business.* Alexandria, VA: Association for Supervision and Curriculum Development.

Livingston, C., & Borko, H. (1989). Expert-novice differences in teaching: A cognitive analysis and implications for teacher education. *Journal of Teacher Education, 40*(4), 36–42.

Maddux, C. D., Samples-Lachman, I., & Cummings, R. E. (1985). Preferences of gifted students for selected teacher characteristics. *Gifted Child Quarterly, 29*(4), 160–163.

Maker, C. J. (1975). *Training teachers for the gifted and talented: A comparison of models.* Reston, VA: Council for Exceptional Children.

Maker, C. J. (1982). *Curriculum development for the gifted.* Rockville, MD: Aspen Systems.

Maker, C. J., & Nielson, A. B. (1996). *Curriculum development and teaching strategies for gifted learners* (2nd ed.). Austin, TX: Pro-Ed.

Manning, M. L., & Baruth, L. G. (1995). *Students at risk.* Boston: Allyn and Bacon.

Marzano, R. J. (2003). *What works in schools: Translating research into action.* Alexandria, VA: Association for Supervision and Curriculum Development.

Marzano, R. J., with Marzano, J. S., & Pickering, D. J. (2003). *Classroom management that works: Research-based strategies for every teacher.* Alexandria, VA: Association for Supervision and Curriculum Development.

Marzano, R. J., Norford, J. S., Paynter, D. E., Pickering, D. J., & Gaddy, B. B. (2001). *A handbook for classroom instruction that works.* Alexandria, VA: Association for Supervision and Curriculum Development.

Marzano, R. J., Pickering, D., & McTighe, J. (1993). *Assessing student outcomes: Performance assessment using the dimensions of learning model.* Alexandria, VA: Association for Supervision and Curriculum Development.

Marzano, R. J., Pickering, D. J., & Pollock, J. E. (2001). *Classroom instruction that works: Research-based strategies for increasing student achievement.* Alexandria, VA: Association for Supervision and Curriculum Development.

Mason, D. A., Schroeter, D. D., Combs, R. K., & Washington, K. (1992). Assigning average-achieving eighth graders to advanced mathematics classes in an urban junior high. *The Elementary School Journal, 92*(5), 587–599.

Mathews, J. (1999, April 20). A call for education change. *The Washington Post,* p. A2.

Matsumura, L. C., Patthey-Chavez, G. G., Valeds, R., & Garnier, H. (2002). Teacher feedback, writing assignment quality, and third-grade students' revision in lower- and higher-achieving urban schools. *Elementary School Journal, 103,* 3–26.

McBer, H. (2000). *Research into teacher effectiveness: A model of teacher effectiveness.* (Research Report #216). Nottingham, England: Department for Education and Employment.

McDermott, P. C., & Rothenberg, J. J. (1999, April). *Teaching in high poverty, urban schools: Learning from practitioners and students.* Paper presented at the annual meeting of the American Educational Research Association, Montreal, Canada.

McLeod, J., Fisher, J., & Hoover, G. (2003). *The key elements of classroom management: Managing time and space, student behavior, and instructional strategies.* Alexandria, VA: Association for Supervision and Curriculum Development.

Meek, C. (2003). Classroom crisis: It's about time. *Phi Delta Kappan, 84*(8), 592–595.

Mendro, R. L. (1998). Student achievement and school and teacher accountability. *Journal of Personnel Evaluation in Education, 12,* 257–267.

Midgley, C., Feldlaufer, H., & Eccles, J. S. (1989). Change in teacher efficacy and student self- and task-related beliefs in mathematics during the transition to junior high school. *Journal of Educational Psychology, 81*(2), 247–258.

Miller, J. W., McKenna, M. C., & McKenna, B. A. (1998). A comparison of alternatively and traditionally prepared teachers. *Journal of Teacher Education, 49*(3), 165–176.

Mitchell, R. D. (1998). World class teachers: When top teachers earn National Board certification, schools—and students—reap the benefits. *The American School Board Journal, 185*(9), 27–29.

Molnar, A., Smith, P., Zahorik, J., Palmer, A., Halbach, A., & Ehrle, K. (1999). Evaluating the SAGE program: A pilot program in targeted pupil-teacher reduction in Wisconsin. *Educational Evaluation and Policy Analysis, 21*(2), 165–178.

Monk, D. H. (1994). Subject area preparation of secondary mathematics and science teachers and student achievement. *Economics of Education Review, 13*(2), 125–145.

Monk, D. H., & King, J. A. (1994). Multilevel teacher resource effects on pupil performance in secondary mathematics and science: The case of teacher subject-matter preparation. In R. G. Ehrenberg (Ed.), *Choices and consequences: Contemporary policy issues in education* (pp. 29–58). Ithaca, NY: ILR Press.

Murnane, R. J. (1985, June). *Do effective teachers have common characteristics? Interpreting the quantitative research evidence.* Paper presented at the National Research Council Conference on Teacher Quality in Science and Mathematics, Washington, DC.

National Academy of Sciences. (2004). *Engaging schools: Fostering high school students' motivation to learn.* Washington, DC: National Academies Press.

National Association of Secondary School Principals (NASSP). (1997). Students say: What makes a good teacher? *Schools in the Middle, 6*(5), 15–17.

National Board for Professional Teaching Standards (NBPTS). (n.d.). *What teachers should know and be able to do.* Retrieved August 21, 2006, from www.nbpts.org/nbpts/standards.

National Center for Education Statistics (NCES). (1992). *Adult literacy in America.* Washington, DC: U.S. Department of Education.

National Center for Education Statistics (NCES). (1997). *Time spent teaching core academic subjects in elementary schools: Comparisons across community, school, teacher, and student characteristics.* Washington, DC: U.S. Department of Education.

National Center for Education Statistics (NCES). (2000). *Monitoring quality: An indicators report.* Washington, DC: Author.

National Center for Education Statistics (NCES). (2004). *The condition of education 2004.* Washington, DC: Author.

National Commission on Excellence in Education. (1983). *A nation at risk: An imperative for educational reform.* Washington, DC: Author.

National Partnership for Teaching in At-Risk Schools. (2005). *Qualified teachers for at-risk schools: A national imperative.* Washington, DC: Author.

National Research Council. (1999). *How people learn: Bridging research and practice.* Washington, DC: National Academy Press.

National Research Council. (2000). *How people learn: Brain, mind, experience, and school.* Washington, DC: National Academy Press.

Neilsen, L. (1999). To be a good teacher: Growing beyond the garden path. *The Reading Teacher, 44,* 152–153.

Nelson, C., & Prindle, N. (1992). Gifted teacher competences: Ratings by rural principals and teachers compared. *Journal for the Education of the Gifted, 15*(4), 357–369.

Neuman, S. B. (2003). From rhetoric to reality: The case for high-quality compensatory prekindergarten programs. *Phi Delta Kappan, 85*(4), 286–290.

Nikakis, S. (2002). What makes an expert teacher of the gifted? *Learning Matters, 7*(1), 42–44.

No Child Left Behind Act, 20 U.S.C. § 6301 (2002).

Noddings, N. (2005, September). What does it mean to educate the whole child? *Educational Leadership, 63*(1), 8–13.

North Carolina Department of Public Instruction. (2000). *Closing the achievement gap: Views from nine schools.* Raleigh, NC: Author.

Nye, B., Konstantopoulos, S., & Hedges, L. V. (2004). How large are teacher effects? *Educational Evaluation and Policy Analysis, 26*(3), 237–257.

Olson, L. (1997). *Research notes: Bad news about bad teaching.* Retrieved August 21, 2006, from www.edweek.org/ew/vol-16/19ideas.h16.

Palmer, P. J. (1990, January/February). Good teaching: A matter of living the mystery. *Change, 22*(1), 11–16.

Peart, N. A., & Campbell, F. A. (1999). At-risk students' perceptions of teacher effectiveness. *Journal for a Just and Caring Education, 5*(3), 269–284.

Pogrow, S. (2005). HOTS revisited: A thinking development approach to reducing the learning gap after grade 3. *Phi Delta Kappan, 87*(1), 64.

Porter, A. C., & Brophy, J. (1988, May). Synthesis of research on good teaching: Insights from the work of the institute for research on teaching. *Educational Leadership, 45*(8), 74–85.

Pransky, K., & Bailey, F. (2002). To meet your students where they are you first have to find them: Working with culturally and linguistically diverse at-risk students. *The Reading Teacher, 56*(4), 370–383.

Pressley, M., Raphael, L., Gallagher, J. D., & DiBella, J. (2004). Providence-St. Mel School: How a school that works for African American students works. *Journal of Educational Psychology, 96*(2), 216–235.

Pressley, M., Wharton-McDonald, R., Allington, R., Block, C. C., & Morrow, L. (1998). *The nature of effective first-grade literacy instruction.* (CELA Research Report No. 11007). Albany, NY: Center on English Learning and Achievement.

Price, J. (2000). The effect of portfolio assessment on student achievement. In National Teachers Policy Institute's *What matters most: Improving student achievement. A report connecting findings of the National Teacher Policy Institute to recommendations of the National Commission on Teaching and America's Future* (pp. 49–51). New York: The Teacher's Network-Impact II.

Qu, Y., & Becker, B. J. (2003, April 23). *Does traditional teacher certification imply quality? A meta-analysis.* Paper presented at the annual meeting of the American Educational Research Association, Chicago, IL.

Quek, C. G. (2005). *A national study of scientific talent development in Singapore.* Unpublished doctoral dissertation, The College of William and Mary, Williamsburg, Virginia.

Randall, R., Sekulski, J. L., & Silberg, A. (2003). *Results of direct instruction reading program evaluation longitudinal results: First through third grade, 2002–2003.* Milwaukee, WI: University of Wisconsin-Milwaukee. Available: www.uwm.edu/News/PR/04.01/DI_Final_Report_2003.pdf.

Rash, P. K., & Miller, A. D. (2000, April). A survey of the practices of teachers of the gifted. *Roeper Review, 22*(3), 192–194.

Reis, S. M., & Small, M. A. (2001). Gifted and talented learners: Many, varied, unique, and diverse. In F. A. Karnes & S. M. Bean (Eds.), *Methods and materials for teaching the gifted and talented* (pp. 1–42). Waco, TX: Prufrock Press.

Reis, S. M., & Westberg, K. L. (1994). The impact of staff development on teachers' ability to modify curriculum for gifted and talented students. *Gifted Child Quarterly, 38,* 127–135.

Renzulli, J. S. (1968). Identifying key features in programs for the gifted. *Exceptional Children, 35,* 217–221.

Renzulli, J. S. (1997). The multiple menu model: A successful marriage for integrating content and process. *NASSP Bulletin, 81*(587), 51–58.

Renzulli, J. S. (1999). What is this thing called giftedness, and how do we develop it? A twenty-five year perspective. *Journal for the Education of the Gifted, 23*(1), 3–54.

Rosenshine, B. V. (1986, April). Synthesis of research on explicit teaching. *Educational Leadership, 43*(7), 60–69.

Rosenshine, B., & Stevens, R. (1986). Teaching functions. In M. C. Wittrock (Ed.), *Handbook of research on teaching* (3rd ed., pp. 376–391). New York: Macmillan.

Rowan, B., Chiang, F. S., & Miller, R. J. (1997). Using research on employees' performance to study the effects of teachers on students' achievement. *Sociology of Education, 70,* 256–284.

Sabers, D. S., Cushing, K. S., & Berliner, D. C. (1991). Differences among teachers in a task characterized by simultaneity, multidimensionality, and immediacy. *American Educational Research Journal, 28*(1), 63–88.

Sanders, M., & Jordan, W. (2000). Student-teacher relations and academic achievement in high school. In M. Sanders (Ed.), *Schooling students placed at risk: Research, policy, and practice in education of poor and minority adolescents* (pp. 65–82). Mahwah, NJ: Erlbaum Associates.

Schalock, D., Schalock, M., & Myton, D. (1998). Effectiveness—along with quality—should be the focus. *Phi Delta Kappan, 79*(6), 468–470.

Scherer, M. (2001, May). Improving the quality of the teaching force: A conversation with David C. Berliner. *Educational Leadership, 58*(8), 6–10.

Seeley, K. (1989). Facilitators for the gifted. In J. Feldhusen, J. VanTassel-Baska, & K. Seeley (Eds.), *Excellence in educating the gifted* (pp. 279–298). Denver, CO: Love Publishing Company.

Senge, P., Cambron-McCabe, N., Lucus, T., Smith, B., Dutton, J., & Kleiner, A. (2000). *Schools that learn: A fifth discipline fieldbook for educators, parents, and everyone who cares about education.* New York: Doubleday.

Shellard, E., & Protheroe, N. (2000). Effective teaching: How do we know it when we see it? *The Informed Educator Series.* Arlington, VA: Educational Research Service.

Shen, J., Mansberger, N. B., & Yang, H. (2004). Teacher quality and students placed at risk: Results from the Baccalaureate and Beyond Longitudinal Study 1993–97. *Educational Horizons, 82*(3), 226–235.

Shernoff, D. J., Csikszentmihalyi, M., Schneider, B., & Shernoff, E. S. (2003). Student engagement in high school classrooms from the perspective of flow theory. *School Psychology Quarterly, 18*(2), 158–176.

Shore, B. M., & Delcourt, M. A. B. (1996). Effective curricular and program practices in gifted education and the interface with general education. *Journal for the Education of the Gifted, 20,* 138–154.

Shulman, L. S. (1987). Knowledge and teaching: Foundations of the new reform. *Harvard Educational Review, 57*(93), 1–22.

Silverman, L. (1995, November/December/January). How are gifted teachers different from other teachers? (Abstract). *The Kaleidoscope, 1,* 8–9.

Singham, M. (2001). The achievement gap. *Phi Delta Kappan, 84,* 586.

Slavin, R. E., Karweit, N. L., & Madden, N. A. (1989). *Effective programs for students at risk.* Boston: Allyn and Bacon.

Snipes, J., Doolittle, F., & Herlihy, C. (2002). *Foundations for success: Case studies of how urban school systems improve student achievement.* Washington, DC: Council of the Great City Schools.

Sokal, L., Smith, D. G., & Mowat, H. (2003). Alternative certification teachers' attitudes toward classroom management. *The High School Journal, 86*(3), 8–16.

Southeast Center for Teaching Quality (SECTQ). (2003). How do teachers learn to teach effectively? Quality indicators from quality schools. *Teaching Quality in the Southeast: Best Practices and Policies, 7*(2), 1–2.

Southern Regional Education Board. (1999). *Getting beyond talk: Staff leadership needed to improve teacher quality.* Atlanta, GA: Educational Benchmark 2000 Series.

Stahl, R. J. (1994). *Using "think-time" and "wait-time" skillfully in the classroom. ERIC Digest.* Bloomington, IN: ERIC Clearinghouse for Social Studies/Social Science Education. (ERIC Document Reproduction Service No. ED 370 885)

Starko, A. J., & Schack, G. D. (1989). Perceived need, teacher efficiency, and teacher strategies for the gifted and talented. *Gifted Child Quarterly, 33,* 118–122.

Stephens, A. D. (2003, September). *The relationship between National Board certification for teachers and student achievement.* Unpublished doctoral dissertation, University of South Carolina, Columbia.

Sternberg, R. J. (2003). What is an "expert student?" *Educational Researcher, 32*(8), 5–9.

Sternberg, R. J., & Grigorenko, E. L. (2002, Fall). The theory of successful intelligence as a basis for gifted education. *Gifted Child Quarterly, 46*(4), 265–277.

Stone, J. E. (2002). *The value added achievement gains of NBPTS-certified teachers in Tennessee: A brief report.* Retrieved August 21, 2006, from www.education-consumers.com/briefs/stoneNBPTS.shtm.

Story, C. M. (1985). Facilitator of learning: A micro-ethnographic study of the teacher of the gifted. *Gifted Child Quarterly, 29,* 155–159.

Strauss, R. P., & Sawyer, E. A. (1986). Some new evidence on teacher and student competencies. *Economics of Education Review, 5,* 41–48.

Stronge, J. H., McColskey, W., Ward, T. J., Tucker, P. D., Howard, B., Lewis, K., et al. (2005). *A comparison of National Board certified teachers and non-National Board certified teachers: Is there a difference in teacher effectiveness and student achievement?* Arlington, VA: National Board for Professional Teaching Standards.

Stronge, J. H., Tucker, P. D., & Ward, T. J. (2003, April). *Teacher effectiveness and student learning: What do good teachers do?* Paper presented at the American Educational Research Association Annual Meeting, Chicago, IL.

Struck, J. M., & Little, C. A. (2003). Making appropriate instructional choices. In J. VanTassel-Baska & C. A. Little (Eds.), *Content-based curriculum for high-ability learners* (pp. 278–304). Waco, TX: Prufrock Press.

Success for All Foundation. (1998). *A proven school wide program for the elementary grades: Success for all.* [Brochure]. Baltimore: Author.

Taylor, B. M., Pearson, P. D., Clark, K. F., & Walpole, S. (1999). Center for the Improvement of Early Reading Achievement: Effective schools/accomplished teachers. *The Reading Teacher, 53*(2), 156–159.

Taylor, B. M., Pearson, P. D., Peterson, D. S., & Rodriquez, M. C. (2003). Reading growth in high-poverty classrooms: The influence of teacher practices that encourage cognitive engagement in literary learning. *The Elementary School Journal, 104*(1), 121–135.

Taylor, B., Pressley, M., & Pearson, D. (2000). *Effective teachers and schools: Trends across recent studies.* Retrieved August 21, 2006, from http://education.umn.edu/CI/taylor/Files/EfftTchrspaper.pdf.

Teddlie, C., & Stringfield, S. (1993). *Schools make a difference: Lessons learned from a ten-year study of school effects.* New York: Teachers College Press.

Tell, C. (2001, February). Appreciating good teaching: A conversation with Lee Shulman. *Educational Leadership, 58*(5), 6–11.

Thomas, J. A., & Montgomery, P. (1998). On becoming a good teacher: Reflective practice with regard to children's voices. *Journal of Teacher Education, 49*(5), 372–380.

Thomas B. Fordham Foundation. (1999). *The teachers we need and how to get more of them.* Retrieved August 21, 2006, from www.edexcellence.net/library/teacher.html.

Tobin, K. (1980). The effect of an extended teacher wait-time on science achievement. *Journal of Research in Science Teaching, 17,* 469–475.

Tobin, K., & Capie, W. (1982). Relationships between classroom process variables and middle school science achievement. *Journal of Experimental Psychology, 74,* 441–454.

Tomlinson, C. (1999). *The differentiated classroom: Responding to the needs of all learners.* Alexandria, VA: Association for Supervision and Curriculum Development.

Tomlinson, C. A. (2000, September). Reconcilable differences: Standards-based teaching and differentiation. *Educational Leadership, 58*(1), 6–11.

Tomlinson, C. A. (2001). *How to differentiate instruction in mixed-ability classrooms* (2nd ed.). Alexandria, VA: Association for Supervision and Curriculum Development.

Tomlinson, C. A. (2003). *Differentiation of instruction in the early grades. ERIC Digest.* Washington, DC: ERIC Clearinghouse on Teaching and Teacher Education. (ERIC Document Reproduction Service No. ED 443 572)

Tomlinson, C. A., & Allan, S. D. (2000). *Leadership for differentiating schools and classrooms.* Alexandria, VA: Association for Supervision and Curriculum Development.

Tomlinson, C. A., Moon, T. R., & Callahan, C. M. (1998). How well are we addressing academic diversity in the middle school? *Middle School Journal, 29*(3), 3–11.

Tomlinson, C. A., Tomchin, E. M., Callahan, C. M., Adams, C. M., Pizzat-Tinnin, P., Cunningham, C. M., et al. (1994). Practices of preservice teachers related to gifted and other academically diverse learners. *Gifted Child Quarterly, 38,* 106–114.

Traina, R. P. (1999). What makes a good teacher? *Education Week, 18*(19), 34.

Tschannen-Moran, M. (2000, Spring). The ties that bind: The importance of trust in schools. *Essentially Yours, 4,* 1–5.

Tschannen-Moran, M., Hoy, A. W., & Hoy, W. K. (1998). Teacher efficacy: Its meaning and measure. *Review of Educational Research, 68*(2), 202–248.

Tucker, P. D., & Stronge, J. H. (2005). *Linking teacher evaluation and student achievement.* Alexandria, VA: Association for Supervision and Curriculum Development.

U.S. Department of Education. (2004). *Meeting the highly qualified teachers challenge: The secretary's third annual report on teacher quality.* Washington, DC: Author.

Vaille, W., & Quigley, S. (2002). *Selective students' views of the essential characteristics of effective teachers.* Retrieved August 21, 2006, from www.aare.edu.au/02pap/via02437.htm.

Vandevoort, L. G., Amrein-Beardsley, A., & Berliner, D. C. (2004). National Board certified teachers and their students' achievement. *Educational Policy Analysis Archives, 12*(46), 1–117.

VanTassel-Baska, J. (1993, July/August). Linking curriculum development for the gifted to school reform and restructuring. *Gifted Child Today, 16*(4), 34–37.

Van Tassel-Baska, J. (1998). The development of academic talent: A mandate for educational best practice. *Phi Delta Kappan, 79*(10), 760–764.

VanTassel-Baska, J. (2005). *Lessons learned from curriculum differentiation, instruction, and assessment.* Presentation at the National Curriculum Network Conference, Williamsburg, VA.

VanTassel-Baska, J., & Little, C. (2003). *Content-based curriculum for high-ability learners.* Waco, TX: Prufrock Press.

Vaughn, S., Bos, C. S., & Schumm, J. S. (2000). *Teaching exceptional, diverse, and at-risk students in the general education classroom* (2nd ed.). Boston: Allyn and Bacon.

Virshup, A. (1997, November 9). Grading teachers. *The Washington Post Magazine: A Special Issue about Education,* 14–17, 31–34.

Wahlage, G., & Rutter, R. (1986). *Evaluation of model program for at-risk students.* Paper presented at the annual meeting of the American Educational Research Association, San Francisco.

Walberg, H. J. (1984, May). Improving the productivity of America's schools. *Educational Leadership, 41*(8), 19–27.

Walberg, H. J. (1986) Synthesis of research on teaching. In M. C. Whittrock (Ed.). *Handbook of research on teaching* (pp. 214–229) (3rd ed). New York: Macmillan.

Walberg, H. J. (1994). Educational productivity: Urgent needs and new remedies. *Theory into Practice, 33*(2), 75–82.

Walker, M. H. (1998, May). 3 basics for better student output. *Education Digest, 63*(9), 5–18.

Walker-Dalhouse, D. (2005). Discipline: Responding to socioeconomic and racial differences. *Childhood Education, 82*(1), 24–30.

Walls, R. T., Nardi, A. H., von Minden, A. M., & Hoffman, N. (2002). The characteristics of effective and ineffective teachers. *Teacher Education Quarterly, 29*(1), 39–48.

Walsh, J. A., & Sattes, B. D. (2005). *Quality questioning: Research-based practice to engage every learner.* Thousand Oaks, CA: Corwin Press.

Wang, M., Haertel, G. D., & Walberg, H. (1993). Toward a knowledge base for school learning. *Review of Educational Research, 63*(3), 249–294.

Wang, M. C., Haertel, G. D., & Walberg, H. J. (1993/1994, December/January). What helps students learn? *Educational Leadership, 51*(4), 74–79.

Waxman, H., Shwu-Yong, H., Anderson, L., & Weinstein, T. (1997). Classroom process differences in inner city elementary schools. *Journal of Educational Research, 97*(1), 1–17.

Weiss, I. R., & Pasley, J. D. (2004, March). What is high-quality instruction? *Educational Leadership, 61*(5), 24–28.

Wenglinsky, H. (2000). *How teaching matters: Bringing the classroom back into discussions of teacher quality.* Princeton, NJ: Millikan Family Foundation and Educational Testing Service.

Wenglinsky, H. (2002). How schools matter: The link between teacher classroom practices and student academic performance. *Education Policy Analysis Archives, 10*(12). Retrieved August 21, 2006, from http://epaa.asu.edu/epaa/v10n12/.

Wenglinsky, H. (2004). Closing the racial achievement gap: The role of reforming instructional practices. *Education Policy Analysis Archives, 12*(64). Retrieved August 21, 2006, from http://epaa.asu.edu/epaa/v12n64/.

Wentzel, K. R. (1997). Student motivation in middle school: The role of perceived pedagogical caring. *Journal of Educational Psychology, 89*(3), 411–419.

Wentzel, K. (2002). Are effective teachers like good parents? Teaching styles and student adjustment in early adolescence. *Child Development, 73,* 287–301.

Westberg, K., & Archambault, F. (1997, Winter). A multi-site case study of successful classroom practices for high ability students. *Gifted Child Quarterly, 41*(1), 42–51.

Westberg, K., Archambault, F., Dobyns, S., & Salvin, T. (1993). The classroom practices observation study. *Journal for the Education of the Gifted, 16*(2), 120–146.

Whalen, S. P. (1998). Flow and the engagement of talent: Implications for secondary schooling. *NASSP Bulletin, 82*(595), 22–37.

Wharton-McDonald, R., Pressley, M., & Hampston, J. M. (1998). Literacy instruction in nine first-grade classrooms: Teacher characteristics and student achievement. *The Elementary School Journal, 99*(2), 101–128.

Whitlock, M. S., & Ducette, J. P. (1989). Outstanding and average teachers of the gifted: A comparative study. *Gifted Child Quarterly, 33,* 15–21.

Wiggins, G., & McTighe, J. (1998). *Understanding by design.* Alexandria, VA: Association for Supervision and Curriculum Development.

Willard-Holt, C. (2003, October). Raising expectations for the gifted. *Educational Leadership, 61*(2), 72–75.

Williams, B. (2003). *Closing the achievement gap: A vision for changing beliefs and practices* (2nd ed.). Alexandria, VA: Association for Supervision and Curriculum Development.

Wilson, S. M., Floden, R., & Ferrini-Mundy, J. (2001). *Teacher preparation research: Current knowledge, gaps, and recommendations. A research report prepared for the U.S. Department of Education.* Seattle, WA: Center for the Study of Teaching and Policy, University of Washington.

Wise, A. E. (2000, Winter). Teacher quality for the new millennium. *The State Education Standard,* 28–30.

Wolk, S. (2002). *Being good: Rethinking classroom management and student discipline.* Portsmouth, NH: Heinemann.

Wong, H. K., & Wong, R. T. (1998). *The first days of school: How to be an effective teacher.* Mountain View, CA: Harry K. Wong Publications, Inc.

Worley, B. B. (2006). *Talent development in the performing arts: Identifying characteristics, behaviors, and classroom practices of effective teachers.* Unpublished doctoral dissertation, The College of William and Mary, Williamsburg, Virginia.

Wright, S. P., Horn, S. P., & Sanders, W. L. (1997). Teacher and classroom context effects on student achievement: Implications for teacher evaluation. *Journal of Personnel Evaluation in Education, 11,* 57–67.

Yamaguchi, B. J., Strawser, S., & Higgins, K. (1997). Children who are homeless: Implications for educators. *Intervention in School and Clinic, 33,* 90–97.

Yildirim, A. (2001, April). *Instructional planning in a centralized school system: An assessment of teachers' planning at primary school level in Turkey.* Paper presented at the annual meeting of the American Educational Research Association, Seattle, WA. (ERIC Document Reproduction Service No. ED 453 192)

Zahorik, J., Halbach, A., Ehrle, K., & Molnar, A. (2003, September). Teaching practices for smaller classes. *Educational Leadership, 61*(1), 75–77.

Zeichner, K. M. (2003). Pedagogy, knowledge, and teacher preparation. In B. Williams (Ed.), *Closing the achievement gap: A vision for changing beliefs and practices* (pp. 99–114). (2nd ed.). Alexandria, VA: Association for Supervision and Curriculum Development.

Index

Note: Page references for figures are indicated with an *f* after the page numbers.

About the Author

James H. Stronge is Heritage Professor in the Educational Policy, Planning, and Leadership Area at the College of William and Mary in Williamsburg, Virginia. Among his primary research interests are teacher effectiveness and student success, and teacher and administrator performance evaluation. He has worked with numerous school districts and state and national educational organizations to design and develop evaluation systems for teachers, administrators, superintendents, and support personnel.

He is the author or coauthor of numerous articles, books, and technical reports on teacher quality and performance evaluation. Selected authored, coauthored, and edited books include the following:

- *Evaluating Professional Support Personnel in Education* (Sage Publications, 1991)
- *Evaluating Teaching: A Guide to Current Thinking and Best Practice* (Corwin Press, 1997, 2006)
- *Handbook on Educational Specialist Evaluation* (Eye on Education, 2003)
- *Handbook on Teacher Evaluation* (Eye on Education, 2003)
- *Handbook on Teacher Portfolios for Evaluation and Professional Development* (Eye on Education, 2002)
- *Handbook for Qualities of Effective Teachers* (Association for Supervision and Curriculum Development, 2004)
- *Linking Teacher Evaluation and Student Learning* (Association for Supervision and Curriculum Development, 2005)
- *Qualities of Effective Teachers (1st edition)* (Association for Supervision and Curriculum Development, 2002)
- *Superintendent Evaluation Handbook* (Scarecrow Press, 2003)

• *Teacher Evaluation and Student Achievement* (National Education Association, 2000)

• *The Teacher Quality Index: A Protocol for Teacher Selection* (Association for Supervision and Curriculum Development, 2006)

Dr. Stronge received his doctorate in the area of educational administration and planning from the University of Alabama. He has been a teacher, counselor, and district-level administrator. He can be contacted at The College of William and Mary, School of Education, P.O. Box 8795, Williamsburg, VA 23187-8795; phone: (757) 221-2339; e-mail: jhstro@wm.edu.